Penny Ellis spent her childhood in Singapore and Cyprus. Her whole family became Christians together in Cyprus in 1973 when she was six years old. Being evacuated in 1974, she was influenced to start writing about overcoming fears. Penny gained a theatre studies degree at London University and started a children's theatre company whilst teaching in the East End of London. Creating educational issue-based shows they were invited to perform at police conferences as well as The Royal Festival Hall. Having battled OCD and self-destructive behaviour, she hopes to help others find that there is a life worth living.

For my husband, Mark, thank you for finding me in 2010 and marrying me a year to the day we met and always loving me just as I am. You are the kindest person I have ever met. All my love.

Penny Ellis

A RIVER THROUGH MY DESERT

AUSTIN MACAULEY PUBLISHERS™
LONDON • CAMBRIDGE • NEW YORK • SHARJAH

Copyright © Penny Ellis (2020)

The right of Penny Ellis to be identified as author of this work has been asserted by her in accordance with section 77 and 78 of the Copyright, Designs and Patents Act 1988.

All rights reserved. No part of this publication may be reproduced, stored in a retrieval system, or transmitted in any form or by any means, electronic, mechanical, photocopying, recording, or otherwise, without the prior permission of the publishers.

Any person who commits any unauthorised act in relation to this publication may be liable to criminal prosecution and civil claims for damages.

Austin Macauley is committed to publishing works of quality and integrity. In this spirit, we are proud to offer this book to our readers; however, the story, the experiences, and the words are the author's alone.

A CIP catalogue record for this title is available from the British Library.

ISBN 9781528992404 (Paperback)
ISBN 9781528992411 (ePub e-book)

www.austinmacauley.com

First Published (2020)
Austin Macauley Publishers Ltd
25 Canada Square
Canary Wharf
London
E14 5LQ

Ilse and Brian Ellis, my parents, for their unwavering belief in God and my conversion with them on that yellow mat in Cyprus. For their steadfast faith that God is the answer despite the question and our daily Bible readings as a family. To Holland Park Hall and All Souls Church for the prayers and word of God brought alive by humble mighty men of God, Ivan, Rico, and also Eddy. For the amazing years of friendship and fellowship with Claire. Thank you Heddi. Thank you also to Rohan and Emms, who taught me how much love can be found in a fellowship group and her letters and inspiration. My beautiful Lizzie. Finally, my darling husband for telling me just to get on with my writing. Praise to God, for with God we do not have a past, only a future.

Introduction

This book is called *A River Through My Desert*. It was written when I got to the end of myself and found that only with Jesus is the beginning of everything. My life was broken completely but he found all the pieces and has put me back together mentally, physically, emotionally, financially and spiritually. He is the source and if we seek him, he will wash us whiter than snow. The title comes from Isaiah 35 v7: 'The burning sand will become a pool, the thirsty ground bubbling springs. In the haunts where jackals once lay, grass and reeds and papyrus will grow.' I pray humbly that this book will help others find freedom from their "burning", their "thirst" and the "jackals". I declare over my life that the devil has taken enough. I am the Lords. It is a fight every day to have the courage to walk in freedom and victory as I get so fearful but I say, 'Your Honour is my life Lord.' There is an answer to every question in the Bible and I have finally realised that. Isaiah 43 v19: 'Behold I will do a new thing now it shall spring forth; shall ye not know it? I will even make a way in the wilderness, and rivers in the desert.' John 7 v38: 'Whoever believes in me as scripture has said, rivers of living water will flow from within them.' A river touches places of which its source knows nothing. I wonder as I take my fresh feet forward out of the desert, who will be touched by this book to follow me out of the desert? I may never know but I pray that they will know Jesus as their best friend who if we seek just keeps on adding to our lives. Oh to leave the natural man in the desert, to shed that skin, take the hooks out of our lips and our minds. God can remove the obstacles and if he doesn't, then he can take us around them safely. The obstacles are a matter of indifference to the river that will flow through me as I keep at the source my saviour and my lord. Let us boldly carry his name and put on his seamless cloak of his reputation. To be emancipated out into personality, free of the tyranny of individuality. To be a sanctified soul. I pray that the Lord will prove his consciousness in me .Those of us who have been in the desert have realised it is only in the desert that the expanse of the horizon is wide enough to see the enormity of the vision, so the fact that we find ourselves in the desert God can turn it round for good. Everyone has a future at the cross we now don't have a past only a future and I don't want to be disobedient to the heavenly vision. Miracles do come as we obey. Even the demons believed in Jesus but they didn't obey him. As I put my feet on the floor as I get out of bed, I declare I am credited to righteousness, I know the battle this day will belong to the Lord. I have come out of the Lazarus' grave of my own making. We need to be around people and situations that loosen those bandages. I do not need to live in that stench anymore. The invisible gas thoughts of terror and horrible anxiety. I don't want anyone to walk around with grave bandages on. I was so bound in them but now I have been enfolded in god's love and immersed in his peace. We can leave the dry desert and find life again, our dry bones can come back to life. Ezekiel 37 v5: 'This is what the sovereign Lord says to these bones: I will make breath enter you, and you will come to life.'

Amen.

Chapter 1
Letters

There are so many noises around us each day; however, when we pray, God hears our "noise". It is more beautiful than any sounds as the Holy Spirit "groans" for us. It is a sound we have never heard on this Earth. Imagine that, our prayers translated to God and the angels sing in heaven. I see and feel my Abba Father with me each day in the sounds of creation around me. It says in the Bible that the stars sing, I would love to know what that sounds like. There are signs all around us, they are for our guidance and are his answers. Whichever way we wish to communicate with him, he always answers us. I started to change my thinking, so instead of all the anxious thoughts, I started looking at everyday objects and things around me. We take so much for granted and probably do not notice that much on our rush to the office etc. So a bird reminds me how free I am as I see it flying in the sky. Feathers tell me I'm transformed by tender grace and made whiter than snow. A yellow rose reminds me how cherished I am. Bones (I see them discarded from a take-away) are a waste of our negative thinking, a branch on my face is God's gentle caress and the perfectly painted dots of colour on tiny petals under the leaves of a huge oak tree that no one sees are His acute attention to detail and so surely I can believe his love is perfect and he will take care of all my needs. Change your mind and see how you see things.

I love reading letters. I thought maybe it could be a way to pray as it is something we are used to doing and receiving. I love writing and I've written endless letters of thanks when I visit those abroad or far away. It tells me so much about a moment or a year, an experience re-lived. God always warns us "lest we forget" so why not write to Him? These letters were written over a long period of time and I praise God for another way for me to talk to him. I expect an answer like you would if you had sent a letter and I pray you will experience just how faithful He is in his response to your letter.

Letter One (Asking for Advice)

Dear Lord,

Me again! Thank you as you only give us good things. All good and perfect things come from above so help me to take time to live by taking the "medicine" given to me each day in the word of God. May I keep on believing in this order of living firstly spirit, then mind, then body? I really find this order a bit uncomfortable but I am trying to change my thinking that has been stuck in some sort of dark l place. Help me to trust and act on your promises, so my life can go forward and be worthwhile. Help me Lord to live in the reality of the truth: the exam is passed, so why do I res-it? The battle is yours. The journey has been made so help me to stop repeating the Groundhog Day. Can you advise me how to live in freedom of good things and not abuse or disbelieve. Yes, to stay happy and steady. I am a bit too anxious and could really do with some advice. Thank you.

Letter Two (How can I love you more)

Dear Lord,

Me again! Help me to live simply today and affirm you in moments. To take a breath and just listen. A branch touches my face it is so gentle. It reminds me of your love, that is soft not harsh. I see the wind move between leaves, so tenderly and strong. Yet you know just how much pressure to exert so it doesn't tear the leaf. I am amazed when I look under the branches of large trees and see you have taken enough time to paint minute pink dot on the underbelly of the leaves. You take so much care on such minute things, how much attention you have focused on me and I never appreciated it. You are so tender. You make everything so perfect, your perfect attention to detail. I notice, Lord, you want me to have perfect peace and joy. I know your words are life and hold power when spoken by you. I need to speak out your words so you can hear them and see my heart praising you. 'I am fearfully and wonderfully made.' Help me to let you love me as much as you say you do. As I look at your care in all you have created, I am in awe. Help me to live the right humbleness and not let my pride stop who you want me to be. Lord, all your creation all around, in the dawn of each morning and all the amazing colours I see around me all day long. How your creation inspires me. It inspires me to do the same, so help me use my talents to do my best and perfect my talents for your glory, as you created the best. You only want the best for your children. As all that is created is all so utterly wonderful, so am I because of you. Help me to love as you love me. You created the world so beautifully, I pray I can create what you have called me to be. May I love you more and more each day? Thank you for such a beautiful world.

Letter Three (I want to believe in the victory)

Me again! Thank Lord that is over! It is finished. You had to shout that on the cross yet what overwhelms me is in the Garden, you knew the helpless limitations of our humanity and you overcame and so can I, as this life is just too much. It's like half of me is saying send me, and the other half feels like I can't do it. It is so amazing how I can claim the same power that raised Jesus from the dead. The same power you called for is a present each morning on my bed, as I wake so I can go forward and not let the knot of fears from unconfessed sins or family cycles, maybe, pull me back. I can run in the light, I am not running in the dark as I'm caught in the vice grip of love, not fear. And I've got everything appertaining to life and I'm more beautiful than a rose and I'm free of all those old perceptions. I will remember that all that hurts me from the past is shadows and I'm in the light. The light is always stronger. Please help me to live your courage, not my zone of comfort. Please help me not to limit you within my vision but to live all of you, all for you, Lord. I don't need to limit myself due to low self-esteem.

Letter Four (Asking for courage)

Help me not to lose what I know, we're such forgetful people. Oh Lord, lest I forget, make me tenacious and efficacious. Give me the ability to wait, your timing is so different from mine. A thousand years is likened to one day, but God, help me not to wander in the wilderness for 40 years and not to give up hope, for Joseph kept faithful despite. Help me to do the right thing at the right time and when all those storms hit, to stay in you despite the chaos. Help me to trust whatever I feel to, hold on to how you see me and the situation is in the "big picture". It's a mosaic. All the little bits matter and despite some dark outlines, you fill each piece with colour. Help me to get things done, even when there seems no immediate call, because if I don't, I'll miss out. Help me to stay away from deception and be in your discernment so to be wise and "holy" that isn't a saint "thing". Lord, it's not about the feeling of ardour a feeling of great warmth, but it is about discernment. I need to believe the courage you have already given me. I want to have the attitude of Caleb. So help me not to go back to what I was when you want me to be the real me, and please make me worthy of the life you have called me to lead. It has been so hard to just BELIEVE and not allow myself to be shaken from the firm hope and the vision of my life, as the best is real and though I feel "upside down", I'm finally the right way up and on the shore.

Letter Five (To tell you Lord how thankful I am)

Thanks so much! You died once for me. You didn't have to resist it like an exam that you failed. You won and my head spins with the enormity of what you accomplished. It is total victory. Help me realise that by studying your word consistently, I get to know you are a best friend. May the words of my mouth and the meditations of my heart be pleasing and help me be inductive and deductive, to tell the truth as I live it against the lust of the flesh. Oh thank you for the revelation of the Holy Spirit for without Him, all my efforts are futile. He gives me creativity and inspiration and comfort and peace. May I use all the nine qualities he offers me and not grieve him, for he can't live in me if I'm in a rage, as he lives in calm and order that he brings with him. He lives in me so I can live out the gifts that are already mine. Help me to live by the bricks of justification and sanctification as they mean freedom, joy and peace as a corner is turned. Help me to remember your moments of blessing to me, to stay steadfast as my feelings do not rule but your love does. Oh make me wise, not meaning that I get so knowledgeable and proud, for I rely completely on you. May I act rightly and consistently in all things, in all moments, wherever I am. And not give in to self-defeat or lack of self-respect. Help me not to worry as that blocks imagination. Help me to realise I have to get up and act now, for it is in the doing I can grasp my identity in you, as I live precious moments as my whole life is an act of worship. Yes, I am free to richly enjoy life. I don't need to lock myself up in chains already broken. I stand on the relationship with you, not mistrust, betrayal and jealousy that ruled. I let go of those loves in Jesus' name and believe in your love. Thank you, like the prodigal, I'm back to my first love. Thank you. My relationships with you is hid safe, no one can take it. I want to live in your framework and I'm on the shore off the broken glass. I live by the songs: Trust and Obey, Spirit of the Living God, Oh What Needless Pain We Bear, Beauty for Ashes, and Nothing Is too Difficult for You. I heed your voice. I discern. I am wise. I am sanctified. I want a Moses shiny face, close relationship with you. Even the great prophets needed inspiration and faith. You have erased my past I only have a future. Yes, I can claim this ground. My dreams are true. I am allowed courage and to be consistent. I count my blessings and can't stop thanking you.

Letter Six (Meeting you in my day)

Thank you, Jehovah, you have showered me in light and enfolded me in love and immersed me in peace. As I came through the tube at St James's, I felt you say to me that there is no turning back, that I needed to set my face like a flint and go up to my Jerusalem. May I go on go forward and run with patience and live the hope and not let the sins so easily beset me that strips me of your joy. The devil loves to make us unhappy so I affirm Jesus and live out my dreams. I want to be living life simply and simply live. I live out my dreams in this moment. It's fab that love is spontaneous. Help me to contain and maintain it by being disciplined in thought, word and deed. Words once spoken do make a journey to the heart. Help me to stay away from the water of temptation and to stay on your shore. I think of the disciples they were met by you on the shore, they were in the right place and not too far away to hear you call them. I need to stay away from mediocrity and double standards. I have allowed myself to be so deceived, I have been too trusting and gullible. Jesus, you have overcome the devil. He doesn't have the power to have inroads in my life anymore. I am so pleased you met up with me today and I was ready to hear you. I know you forgive me of my sins yet I know there are consequences. I have been in such dark places because I didn't listen to you. I don't want to be a coward, and I know the power of prayer and if I don't want to risk dying for it than is it worth living for? I want to be a spiritual thermometer for you. The Bible isn't a book, it's a way of life!

Letter Seven (Meeting you in my sleep)

Yippee for victory. Whatever challenges I faced today, I can now lie down and you give the gift of sleep. As I sleep, Lord, keep me in peace tonight and may your Holy Spirit work in me during the night, deep in my subconscious. May he open my heart and fill me with love and strength and truth. I don't ask for deliverance from, but victory is my circumstances. In the morning, Lord, help me to wake refreshed knowing this is the day the Lord has made and I can rejoice and be glad in it. May my first thoughts be of you in the morning dew. Thank you for the gift of sleep that gives me the strength to face a new day and despite the challenges may your glory be revealed. I praise you for your promise of restoring the years the locusts have eaten. I thank you that you have a plan to prosper me. I enlist this suffering that sometimes clouds my mind in the darkness of the night. Let not my heart be troubled in the midnight hours and to claim your promise that all things work together for good and for your glory.

Letter Eight (For setting me free)

Thank you. I now know the things that belong to my peace. I have learnt, Christ. It has taken me a long time but I am so grateful that I am changed! I am inspired by the change you wrought in Jacob. It reminds me of me and I am so humbled. I was here all along. I paint this day yellow! Truth is found in you and I allow myself to choose life. I do not need to self-destruct. Help me to realise the importance of my life and you are the restorer you are not pinching me to remind me of what I have been. You don't shove that in my face, rather you lead me. I don't need to grieve anymore. I want to live in abandonment to you as I do when I'm dancing. I'm free. Yes, I've turned the corner! Perfect love has cast out fear. I've been bought with a price so help me to be holy and honour you with this body. I'm so grateful that even though I'm so alone at times and feel so lonely that you're my Agappi. I mean you love me with such love, I only ever lived Eros love. What a difference is your love. Thank you for the promise of Escatonne and Charismata love. It is a love that I can live in till I die. Your love is amazing. Please continue to change my mind today.

Letter Nine (Embrace the day and expect good things)

Oh God, forgive me for the dullness of my vision and the weakness of my faith and the joylessness of my living. Give my moods a kick, as I live delivered. It's a brand-new day. Good morning, God, and thank you. I can achieve new things today. A day to live. I don't need to binge or waste money or words. I can learn something new about myself. I can love this world as I awake in freedom, peace and joy. Help me to stay in the spirit and not miss out on what is expected of me and what gifts are out there to receive. I remember all the blessings you have given me, help me to take time to have patience, to listen as I invite the Holy Spirit to live in me. Help me to live spirit, then mind, then body. To live in the heavenly realms, not the world's. I'm amazed you have called me by name and you see me. So help me to see me as you see me. At the edge of despair is the limit of the possible, then faith can do its work, wow! Mostly man obeys where there is a need. Thank you, you have taken me aside to rest and reveal your will and let my needs be met to trust you know best. To trust is the hardest so I become a worker with you, not for you. You have shown me what I am without you and let me be available for where you want me to go and what you want me to do today. To be still enough to feel you nudge me or hear your directions. From such small steps of faith, you can work something amazing out. I step out in faith in the character of God and the Holy Spirit has given me common sense to keep me in discerning you. Help me to stop doing things in my own strength like Moses did at times. Today I go step by step with you. Yes, your timing is perfect and you've been preparing me. I look forward to my burning bush directions today!

Letter Ten (That I get up and live a life worth living)

Lord, I ask that I do your will today, that I don't grieve the Holy Spirit, that I live happy and content, not greedy or out of balance. Help me to work out what you have worked in. To live fully alive on this path and to know what to pick up and what to leave behind, so to let my self-respect increase and my creativity. Heal my confidence and communication skills. Dispel the negativity from my mind and surround me with harmony. Help my inner soul's self be in balance with my outer personality. Help me to build strength and courage, grow and progress as a thermostat, not a thermometer. To be creative in my talents and self-confidence, to live, love and be happy and live in the right energy. To have steadfastness to achieve the goals, to live in inspiration and intuition and be successful in outcome. To do my best. I don't care being insignificant but make me be significant for you. Yes, make me useful and positive and purposeful, whole and complete. I want to be full of life and abundantly in the joys of the Lord alone. So I ask this of you in your name only.

Letter 11 (Coming out of a dreadful situation)

On the 5.5.07 you hold me so close. This is a day of order. Help me to hold your vision for my life fast and clear in front of me. To be alive and aware, to have the armour of God on, to live the newness of life and the creativity I see around me as it is for your glory that I now do my best and leave self-destructive habits behind. To do my best with my writing and to keep to the inspirations, to stay steadfast, to keep focused on the inspirations. Oh so many you have given me. To be like others who did it. Like reading about Elisabeth Rooney and your guidance is the poetry of D. L. S. Sayer, her vision and completion of "The Man Born to be King". So help me to leave behind timidity. I need so much love and I've gone down the wrong cul-de-sac. You warn us to stay on the path and not veer to the left or the right. Help me to give you my love and yes, the right love and not to look for it in anyone but you. It is about 100 percent of you, in abandonment. I don't need to live with my feet in people's sympathies, nor be held back by others' insecurities or failing in lust and ego, and how can you give me more if I waste this? He that is in me is greater than he that is in the world.

Letter 12 (Why do I let moods dominate me?)

O Lord, I ask you humbly that I am not to be tossed about by the sins that so easily beset me. It is not the undisciplined nature nor the devil's attacks. It is my moods. I've got to give them a kick. Get this thing off my heel. Why am I causing my own pain and fears when there is no need? I can use the courage to live this risen life. I accept this new life so that I will live risen and abundantly. Let me shake myself so that I find I can do and say what I thought I could not. Possess my soul. I will watch myself. I will fight in the spiritual realm. The chink in my armour can be overcome. I put to death the human passions and desires. Let the spirit control me, not greed or impatience. I can wake up free, not bloated from a binge in fear. It is over. I let go. The best is real and now I'm the real me as my identity is in you.

Letter 13 (Significant moments)

Christmas 1996, I will praise you. You touch me. The snow of Christmas, its depth, the quiet of the snow, as it is floating down on me. I have been washed of my sins and am whiter than snow. You took hold of my hand and led me into the New Year. It is so hard to let you lead me as I can't see the way, yet I trust you. I just keep in the forefront of my mind, the great experiences you have given me. Triumphant living is a moment by moment, daily process. Calm in the chaos. It is your peace I can fix my mind on not letting my imagination run riot. May my mind be stayed on you?

Letter 14 (After rejection)

15th May 1996, as he left again, I did not feel the urge to binge. I felt warm and free. You said to "place your hand just there". I felt you hold me so intimate your love is all I need, and then hearing at church about self-esteem and confidence, how when I see the expectations God has for my life, I feel humanly inadequate, like you did in Gethsemane. You can't do it as in the human strength. So in you, I can do the great things and be who you made me to be. I can experience the great same power that raised Jesus from the dead. You made me creative and beautiful, in you I'm free, and transformed from dark to light. Thank you, Lord, I accept your gifts and believe trial leads to trust and trust to triumph, so I can reclaim the vision of my life and let me not hinder you in the daily living or the indecisiveness and inconsistent actions and thoughts. Help me to stay consistent and clear in my focus of this vision for you.

Letters 15 (A letter of restoration)

Lord, help me to live spirit, mind, then body to be so content, confident and consistent, courageous and creative. To immerse me, Lord, in the overflowing, with the Holy Spirit to equip me to keep walking close to you. I have felt that fingerprint pressed pressure of love, yes your closeness, like washing my face with one of those hot towels. Such deep joy, help me to claim my joy of the Lord, it is my total strength. So I will be confident and full of hope, efficacious and tenacious, connected to the energy and in control, full of hope, and seeing your beauty in all around me and inside and outside of me. So whole, complete, beautiful, stretching my mind and a total recreation, a newness of self of my mind and a consistency I never knew before. I step out in intimacy with you only, and so live such calm order and sanity. At a deeper level so I am equipped to do my best in my attitude, at work and in my stance. Help me to keep in focus. My body is the temple of the living God so help me to be disciplined as it's yours. Help me to stay on the deepest level and to meet you there on that deepest level and so be on fire. To live so is to live simply, yes simply profound, to keep the burning fire of hope and never give in to the darkness around me. To stay in joy and not grieve anymore as the joy of the Lord is my strength. I claim this and live the power of the words as they are living words, they are life itself. I am allowed to be me, and safe as the snow edges confirmed in sharp moonlight rays. We can all be so fulfilled and the best is to be free. Help me to be illuminated, to live the truth of Thess 1 v5: 'to realise and be convicted by the power'. So to keep singing this new song in a new being, so the chains are shadows. Like a ghost, they fall away. I believe your words are life and I claim total victory.

Letter 16 (Remind me your honour is my life)

Each day is great. I can have inner confidence so I can let go of timidity and go for it and make it happen. Yes, I can have the love of the Heavenly Father, the holy love, the intrinsic love. I can have self-discipline to keep control and keep control of self. I can use it. I can say it and live by doing my life. Yes, another brand-new day. Thanks for sewing the sky together for another day to see your splendour in nature and a day nearer coming home to you. Thank you that I can write today that you meet me in the library and encourage me. Oh fill me with wisdom. Yes, I walk on the shore with you and while everyone is just riding the tube, I am speaking to you. It is the dawn rising on this new shore, talking to you. Thank you. I can use my mind in this way. Your love is so holy, give me boldness to use my talents in the right way as you give me this gift of the day. Help me to do in your intimacy only and not waste in timidity, fear and despair, and lack of trust. Keep me near you Lord, walking in truth. Protect me from others' demands of lust and ego. Help me to respect, regard and affirm me as it is over. It is done once and won. Help me to live your honour, trust and understanding. So I live out your insights for my life and I was here all along. You know how to give us good things. So I plant my talents to live conscious reason and will in my behaviour. I realise anger is a gift only to use in danger, not to let sins overtake, but to trust and do.

Letter 17 (Your answers)

Lord, I thank you that in every situation I can only see you Today I chatted about love and I identify with your love and thanks for connecting me to those people I've been praying for. They just rang and we chatted. I realise what walking in faith is and only you have brought order to the areas of my life that no one could help me with. Thank you, Lord, that the strongholds are down and I'm free and I can enjoy even the bubbles in the bath. Help me to just get on with it. It's at times like this that your word is life, a life-line. Yes, Lord, so I fall back on your promises as I pour, the glass appears. Help me to walk with you as Enoch walked with you and I am wise and humble, for we were created to praise you and I glorify you through all I write. May my life be the answer to someone's equation. All of you and none of the self, than I am fully known.

Letter 18 (A Jabez life)

Isn't it so simple yet so profound how when we go deeper with our Lord, we experience the best. Up till then, we have had good stuff but good is not best. I meant to really get to know you Lord, so often in life we think we know someone but really we don't, yet here's our chance to know Jesus. To let God meet the life of a life that is constant with Christ and His power is surprising if we obey the life he has given us. If we are rightly related to him, how he simply will look after us. He always has a 'much more' amount to give us. Keep Him first. Keep up that standard as there is always some mundanity, some quirky or odd ball thing that will roll by. I would say that sometimes I think I'm OK and then I trip up. I can never be off my guard as the closer I try to get to you, the more subtle is Satan's attacks. You have given me the armour, Lord, and I need to put it on. Let this day be full of rest, not impetuousness. I am allowed to be calm, ordered and sane. Thank you for Jabez. Oh I hope we ask for the other half of the blessing to become what God wants, not what I want to get. To not be so uprooted but entwined in the vision of my life. Help me to live what is already won. To know the turtledove of peace is here. I can attack evil with truth. I can stand up under temptation. In Christ, thank you that I can do all things. I can have a vision like Jabez. I can live the much more. I can delight to do your will. Christian living isn't to do something unpleasant; it is a true delight.

Letter 19 (A Caleb attitude)

Help my stance, attitude, perceptions and disposition be all yours God. So often I do let blind panic in and yield and become a slave again to myself. I know there is no power in the human soul of itself to break the bondage of a disposition formed by yielding. I don't need that impetuous; that urge I must have it at once! Once I have yielded, I realise. I can't just give that habit up. There has been sand in my shoes for way too long now. I need to avoid deliberately the paths of self. Just turn away and pass on. I don't want to compromise anymore as I now know black and white are truly different. I can come so far in faith and then be defeated by sand in my shoes. Help me realise the subtlety of the devil. How I will stumble over pebbles, not mountains. I want the mind of my spirit, to be in perfect agreement with the life of the son of God in me. I want to get serious with God and leave the rest alone. I saw how you maintained an inner watchfulness where you submitted your spirit to the Father. I have a responsibility to keep my spirit in agreement with His spirit. May I perfect holiness in the fear of God? I want God to get his way with me. I want to walk and not faint. I want to be tried and proved and, in your strength, I can stand the test. I am so grateful for a way out. That mental despair and lack of faith in myself is over.

Letter 20 (A life worth living)

Thank-you God in (Jeremiah 45.5). You say thy life I will give thee for a prey in all the places whither thou goest. This means you will give me my life wherever I go. I will always come out with my life, forget blessings and wanting things, let me remain in the life hid with Christ in God. Help me not to ask, 'Well, what about this or that?' but to just let go. I am surprised and delighted by the life you, God, have given me back. I step out of the disobedience in thoughts and actions and I am accepting, even on this most simple level. I don't have anyone or anything in my life now that would cause me pain. The struggle and the spirit of poverty is over. I get into the habit of saying 'Speak Lord' and feel your strong hand in the pressure of circumstances. I am certain of my uncertainty. I live in breathless expectation as to the way my days will pass and I do the duty that lies nearest and I know only in you is life spontaneous, joyfully uncertain and full of expectancy. I leave my whole life to you now. I don't go back to what I was. When you, God, want me to be something I've never been, I now know the knowing is in the doing. I know now it is dangerous to lose what I know. Help me Lord, to do things in the right time and to hold on despite what I feel like, and to hold on so tightly to what you see me as. Help me to get it all done even though there seems no immediate call. So I don't lose perception or discernment to stay so centred that nothing rocks me. Not to be deceived by feelings of ardour, feelings that are just great warmth's but make me worthy of the life you have called me to lead, to live simply and simply live.

Letter 21 (How do I walk in the right rhythm?)

Dear God, this walking, running thing is so demanding. Walking in the fast pace, set out in time limits, late for work or rush hour, so called as we want our unpaid time to not be lost in travel. We are all running to meet or sort or finalise or revive or retreat or dissolve something. Are we ever in the stride of God, living at His pace? Oh Lord, I just want to say at last the time is yours. The husk is broken. I am out of individuality and into the personality you set aside for me. The stop and see, the vision in consistency and courage. Like Moses, it's been 40 years in the wilderness. I didn't kill anyone but I did die in myself and destroyed plans, hopes and futures, as I let go in my own indignation, in the spirit of the temperate man. It wasn't the right humbleness; it was a deceived need to please people needing to be needed and to claim their approval so running into debt and debauchery. All I got out of those years was the fact that, like Moses, I'd just been feeding sheep. Now you call me out of that shrunken up life that became smaller than a grain of sand. Only in this desert your call has brought healing and family unity and a calm mind and enlargement and I can take the right stride as God has called me and indeed, I am that I am hath sent me. Now I am still of use, I crave nothing that I used to. I am in harmony at last, like the sound of silence, on top of a snow-covered mountain where sky and mountain join in their immensity. Just simply into clear whiteness. Burn my lips Lord and send me.

Letter 22 (Sing in the ordinary days)

Dear God, I guess we have to get up and eat and drink something. How do we do the ordinary for the glory of God? We stand in so many shallows in our days: phone calls, waiting in queues to pay, and meals we have to eat. I do hope I won't be a spiritual prig by saying I would not be found in the shallow moments. I can be eating, drinking, walking and talking as it is all ordained of God. May I value these moments and sing despite the grey of the day when everything seems like just a chore. May I be safe in the shallows as I apply common sense the common sense from you and please reveal the deeps to me. In all these duties may I praise you and not let any circumstance strip me of your joy. If I stay in the centre of your will, I can still have deep joy. There are many ways I can react today. How often we perform at being real. We put on a smile and have a heart that resents every minute. I hope I can see the deep in the everyday things and run into the ocean of joy despite the limits and dullness of the day. I think it is when we think we deserve something better and forget what we actually have. I want to shed that skin of superficiality and live the bone marrow of salvation and truth and really live it out. I have found the ocean so in this life of shallows I can dive deep.

Letter 23 (To build my character)

Dear God, I'm so grateful how you have pressed me into you. I have indeed felt your weight. To feel you so close, I wonder have I got closer to you or did you come closer to me or have you been that close all along. It's like knowing angels are truly around. We are told angels walk amongst us and we may entertain them unawares. They do come to us in so many ways we all have a guardian angel. They come as: messenger, the deliverer, the audible voice, the burst of energy and enlightenment, the restraining influence, the warming in amongst the compulsive disorder of self-destruction that hiccups my life. You do come down to me level. I know you're with me all day long, you close the corridor windows of my soul. May I know you are indeed all the security I need to stay consistent and to be the realest me as you indeed make the best of me the realest me? You make me into the person I really am as you created me and not others, who try to tell me who I am. You make me realise I can be my very own best friend to myself. I can be a good steward of all I am because of you in my body, mind, in work, in money. All of me can go forward as surviving means I've built character for my next goal in life. I know the clouds have been there for me to unlearn my mistakes, so I can also be disciplined like a warrior in my life. Change doesn't need to scare me as it means I move on to something better, the other side. To know my bent now, that consecrated energy out of the tyranny of individuality I can shout 'out, out, out.' Thank you for sudden discovery as all the pain and inconvenience is instability forgotten. It is an inexpressible find and it is so thrilling to get an answer, an insight into our own make up, to understand the why behind the fear, to have just the right expression to describe a feeling and finding relief from needless guilt. Oh Lord, may I turn my ear to wisdom and apply my heart to understanding. May I look for it as silver, as hidden treasure that I may understand the fear of the Lord and find the knowledge of God as I break into personality and character?

Letter 24 (Letting go)

Dear God, had a Queen of Sheba deep dissatisfaction moment – realising what it is in this world. My heart is indeed restless till it finds its rest in you. I want to be Lemon Zest, sharp in you. Thank you for Caritizo – charismata for escatonne. I am now healed. I can truly taste and see that the Lord is good. That my life can be of use and I can be the answer to someone else's questions. That to live not in habits but free, unlocked from mindsets. To remember my uncertainty comes when I push away and try forgetting the reality of others that I can dance on the shores of life. I have dismounted the tiger. I am covered in your fingerprints. Oh Lord, my God, the nightmare is over. I can renounce strongholds, like a piece of art reflects and says something about the person who created it. So I see your gentleness, your tenderness, a little bit of your majestic. God, in how a bird looks after its young, in the dormouse resting in the peak of a mountain top, that it was for freedom that Christ has set me free. I know my mind is like the entrance to a home. A thought knocks at the door. What do I do? Anxiety weighing a thousand pounds comes in and leaves their burdens. They made an early start, they troop in, but you hold the key and you can lock them out. I remember hell is just so small and giants are way too big to miss and I do have the gift of common sense. May I fight the right battles? Please help me. I need to stay in the places of your safety. You have brought me to a standard. Help me to stay in the places and thoughts that are yours. Wherever I go, you do go with me, like a graph. Just let the feelings go, the anxiety line will come down. I can keep my hands on the plough. I have come back to my senses. I have got 'Benjamin' blessings. I don't need to see the worry in everything anymore. The lies are over. I can go where no settlers have gone. To discover the depth, width, breathe, length of priceless love in you.

Letter 25 (Coming out the other side)

Dear God, I survived the shipwreck. I was on sins jagged reefs but I saw the land of shining shores and when I came onto land from the shipwreck, kings shut their mouths on account of you in me. I was off course without heeding and I wandered off into jeopardy and risk, now torn clothes of self are healed as whiter than white. The blood has said it all now. My heart, mind, body is seamless, is totally whole. The cross has said it all. Up there, humanity is on full display. I know the gospel painter sort of airbrushes your agonising vigil in the Garden of Gethsemane. You were alone and trembling, surrounded by sleepy disciples and desperately praying. You really did know what it was like to be human. We see a mere snapshot but in reality, like us in our fearful moments, we don't want to be in solitude. We don't want that cold realisation in our own aloneness of the sheer horror. You even cracked open a window to reveal the state of your soul. What amazes me, Lord, is how you fell to the ground and in the Garden, that verb is in the Greek, is the imperfect tense suggesting a continual action. That you literally kept falling to the ground. The wrath of God was turned loose on you! You kept falling so we don't have to. I don't need to fall into worldly wisdom, or inferiority or dependency or materialism. Lord, I know I love you so much more than the things I fear you met me at midnight and took me out of my nightmares. May I turn my face to my destiny now in Gethsemane, Lord? I find out who I am. But despite the terror, it also is tranquil. The terror is I'm not in control of my life or those I love. The tranquillity comes when I remember you are in control. Nothing need pin me to a cold, hard floor. The victory in heaven is in the surrender of the human soul and if I courageously surrender and not to struggle, all will be well.

Letter 26 (God shaped)

Dear God, I get that realisation of how I need you. You have the perfect timing. I come to grips with my own weakness because humility comes before honour. Lord, may the intensity of my resolve and in the divine moments not evaporate in the cold, ordinary days. May I look on you and know your approved look on me, that I take up my cross each day, that my hands are full of you. I have let fear of rejection and believing I actually needed the lies. The lack of identity in my God shape allowed me to compromise. I want to walk in the God stride and talk and dance for you, to hold onto the rainbow handle of peace and promises, to do and not deny, to pour and the glass comes. Let people see it is your joy, not my craziness, that I stay in the link of body and believers that you are with me till the end of the age. That you alone are the answer to my equation. In this world, everything solid turns to sand. I don't want to walk anymore with sand in my shoes. You went before. You have been in all my situations. You went before Annas, then Caiaphas, then the council of elders, then Pilate, then Pilate again. Their dilemma was how they would convict an innocent man. So I can stand up before anything, anyone. Stand in front of anyone as you stand in front of me. I take the sand out of my shoes. May I be in regal dignity, silent and composed as the paradox of salvation was from acts of injustice? The justice of God was satisfied.

Letter 27 (What freedom is)

Dear God, the wonders of freedom. I was sitting on my own death row in sins so dreadful. I was in ultimate despair but now I am called out of prison, like Barabbas, out of death, off death row by my name and I am released. I am realising, God, how I missed my cross because of you. Now I can go higher till I don't see or hear all the situations, the comments and the compromises. I know no one has or will do such an immense act of love for me as you did. Thank-you Jesus – tetelestai 'it is finished' through the cross. I am cut and implanted with order, sanity and holiness in my nerves, mind and heart. Your back was ripped up for me. You now have got my back! I keep on saying your prayers. I repeat the truth daily. I grasp it so I do the truth. Let me follow the way of freedom in a spirit refined only by you. Let me live a better way of living. Let you alone fill my thirst. I know no one is ever too far gone to become a Christian. It is my sin that holds you on the cross where you can't move where you have to accept everything done to you so that I can move and live and breathe and have my being so freely. You were held, fixed, so

I could be free! You know what it was like to scream, 'My God, why have you forsaken me.' The word "anaboan" means to scream out. I scream sometimes. I know you hear my heart's screams and understand them.

Letter 28 (The cross has said it all)

Dear God, it's amazing to think how you became human. I mean I am always going to be human till I die, then I get an immortal body. What a fab makeover that is going to be. You were theanthropic – Theos = God anthropos = man, and on the cross you were actually thirsty. In the desert you started your ministry 40 days hungry and you end it thirsty. You had no one. You knew what it's like to have loneliness and hurts, you understand us intimately because our doubts, our insecurities, our disillusionments, never slip past you unnoticed. Hope deferred maketh the heart sick but desire fulfilled is a tree of life! I love it when you shouted your victory shout on the cross 'It is finished.' You had done it. You had realised God's desire and how amazing that feels to be in God's perfect plan at the right place in obedience. I love that victory shout when I know I've done God's will, totally. You used an everyday expression. You kept it so immediate and real. "Tetelestai" was said frequently in those days so anyone hearing you shout would know it as a positive comment! And with that, you tore through the heavy veil of death's darkness for us. Now the devil is one day closer to the end! Now I can put the cross before me. I can get that close to you God and no one can get to me as the cross protects my way. The safest place to be is in the centre of God's will.

Letter 29 (Following your example)

Dear God, just thinking a lot in these letters of the life I can actually have because of your death. And how tenderly you died in the sense of how tender you were in what you said before you died. You said "father" – how close was your communication with God throughout all your ordeal in the Garden and when you were nailed up, you called out "father".

That is who you committed yourself to like we need to do "into your hands". Yes, you put yourself in God's hands. Godless men might have held your captive sinful hands betrayed you. They slapped and bound you but you acted by voluntarily committing your spirit to the father's care, with childlike confidence. There is no uncertainty when we go through death because you have taken all of that away. I am not hopelessly plunged in it but a peaceful trust of course my words are not infallible. My words aren't miraculous. My character isn't perfect. But still our mutual suffering links my heart to yours on a deeply human level. You understand the depth of my pain. You learnt obedience while you were here. You learnt how to obey to the point of suffering! Pain deepens my trust in you, Lord. My faith will only remain shallow if it isn't tested. Can I learn obedience to be silent and patient and not insult when I've been criticised, to fiercely cling to the father's will when people try to get rid of me. And you know what it was like to experience God's silence. Can I do the same! Only it seems it is in pain do people fall on their knees and reconsider life. What severe lessons will I learn from? I hope I can follow your example.

Letter 30 (You call my name)

Dear God, just looking at another dawn, they are all so different. Different shades of colour as the brightest light rises into the sky. Sometimes there is just a glimmer on the horizon. It reminds me that death no longer has the last word. Life now has the final say! We may follow a dead hero into death but it's our living saviour that can usher us back into life again. That ton weight of stone was rolled away. How much weight do we need to shift mentally or because of the consequences of our lives in order to let the risen saviour through? It is even as we dare to believe yet run to see! If only we would stop and listen. For like Jesus did, he called out 'Mary' she was in a place where she could meet him and tuned in enough to recognise his voice. We need to make sure we're in the places God can meet us. God can call us by our name. Hope we haven't gone so inward after disappointing events, that we don't hear Him call. Has there been that season, like the disciples had once the crucifixion had happened. Where we go, all aimless and disillusioned and frightened. Then one day we realise just how free we are in a risen life and that how we change from sheep to roaring lions. We don't need to be in conflict with our mortality. We can face our humanity. It's up to us. The quality we live by. Jesus has called us out of the tomb but then it's up to us to take off the bandages of death, the stench of life, not lived and live! I'm so glad I can experience strength restored and a renewed relationship with God. So I can walk into the day as the dawn awakes, the sun rises. I can be part of the start of a whole new day.

Letter 31 (Getting over OCD and wrong thinking)

Dear God, just thinking about the power of the mind and all its pretensions that set themselves up against the knowledge of God and we take captive every thought to make it obedient to Christ. The weapons we fight with are not the weapons of the world. On the contrary, they have divine power to demolish strongholds. We demolish arguments and realise, God, that the carefully planned strategy the devil prepares us as we wake up, they are already meticulously planned carefully, coordinated and He will flawlessly execute them. We battle in the spiritual and it is where eternity is won or lost in us. I realise I need to brace myself each morning so I don't have division or bitterness or lovelessness and an apathetic spirit of defeat. I need to get up and plant Christ' flag in the fortress of my mind. To let the Holy Spirit bathe me and to re-pattern my whole way of thinking, to align my mind with the mind of Christ. All the bits that life throws at me, I can toss over my shoulder and put behind bars! I don't want to be edged away from the light and put out into nothing and realise I've taken the wrong turning and now I'm heading in the opposite direction on a motorway I can't get off. It's like going through your wardrobe and discarding all the t-shirts with slogans: "you're to blame", "you're a joke", "you're a burden", "you're a liability", "you're selfish". It's getting up and rearranging the mental furniture from the night before to have it around Jesus. I think I carry one of the lightest hearts around with me, not full up, except with light and love and joy.

Letter 32 (I am clearing the garden)

Dear God, can you burn my lips, erase black thoughts, pull out the roots, weed me out. What seeds have I planted now that rise up and choke me. They were bought in a packet called compromise! I need to uproot those stubborn, mental weeds. I don't need every day to be so cluttered and tangled. It's so nice to have my brick work in secure order, all my bricks, the wall I lean against that protects me from the elements. Each brick is a person in my life who picks me up, loves me unconditionally. God, I want you to be my modern, mighty hero. I want to have reverent fear and respect for your word. I want to be hand held up truth that the seeds I plant will grow up and change landscapes! You want me to be the apple of your eye. I lay hold of the truth today, grab it and hold on. I want to tattoo it on my heart. The truth is bigger than the giants and they are too big to miss. I want to stay sharp, razor sharp, and use my adrenaline for God. To get dressed in my best for Him each morning. I am so grateful you have given me my heavenly birthright and I can live in the blueprint of my destiny. Like lightening that displays its brightest, white strength without a sound. Your kingdom offers power in your words! I know my stump is still there now the roots have found their source. I secure the stump with a band of iron and bronze and let it be drenched by the dew. I break off the dead twigs. I break away from the sins. I've had enough of pig swill or eating grass like Nebuchadnezzar did. Instead I am lifted up once again. And despite limits, I am on the right road going the right way and given the keys to the kingdom. A purpose and a plan are mine now.

Letter 33 (Can I be in the centre of your will?)

Dear God, it is indeed the tone that creates the music. I want to be more centrifugal. Yet I want to hold onto God's spiritual kingdom that it will dilute the worldly philosophies and purify the polluted tributaries of our mind. Can I let you call the shots in my life? Can I make you first? I don't want to bury my one talent ever again. I want to use it for your glory. I can get up each day and be in a party, a celebration of life dressed in my best. May the intentions of my heart be right? I don't want to live in the gall of bitterness. I want to take home the trophy and display it with all confidence that you, Lord, won the match. I was thinking, do I model discipline in the small corners of my life, where the camera lights aren't blaring and no one will see. Can I just see the bigger picture or am I too immediate and erratic just jumping into the feel good moments. I always wonder and get myself in check with the idea, am I tickled by the world or hand held in your blueprint. It's remembering that the truths are hidden in my heart and the devil truly can't find them, so why be afraid. I want to be bold, to nail a godly life to the wall and live in the frame despite feeling frayed. It is time that I had enough faith and bought the field and lived out the victory a most glorious victorious life.

Letter 34 (Scent of God)

Dear God, so glad to be committed to you in a world full of uncertainties. I give you my heart, my all, as you are my creator and if nothing else, I know where I have come from, who I am in you and where I will end, end of job done. Hurrah! Anything that jars with my love for you if it clashes, I just don't need it. It truly is that simple. It is how loosely I can hold everything else. A loose grip on the life that is mine as I hold tightly to you, I face the outer world, my inner self and the devil himself, daily. Not living by limitations or fears with the right respect for myself. Like I execute the waste of my life and put the rest of self to death too, as after comes new life, like you Lord. I come out of a cold tomb of limitations into newness of life, full of a living way. Do people realise that they are in a calling, that they have an anointing. It isn't just the people in the Bible it happened to. We are still called today and that extraordinary life can be lived out by us today. Heaven, like a chemistry set, takes all my bits, all my past and all my thoughts and reshapes them all into the gold shape I was always meant to be. I want to live in the scent of heaven for heaven has come down today and not in the stench of the world that grapples for meaning. I want to know my smell in you. I want to know the smell of Jesus.

Letter 35 (Am I climbing the right mountain?)

Dear God, am I just climbing on a climbing frame or have I finally got to the mountain and have started to tackle the steep, sheer mountain side. What was I worrying about all these years that knotted and tied me into the climbing frame of a child's playground? I was so emotionally sensitive, continually trying to please the world's expectations, desperate for any attention and approval from people that ended up deceiving me. I never was looking up high enough to see, never seeing the better real heights to climb that would matter and make a difference. Do I now live above the level of mediocrity and how long would it take me to see your works: your miracles. I think I sort of do now after wasting about 30 years, I can finally say: 'I was here all along!' So much of what you want for me to be, is finished and fully furnished. All I need do is climb up the right way to get in. I feel I am starting to do that and miracles are unfolding before my eyes! I think because I now don't compare myself to anyone or let anyone's comments stick, I am emancipated out into personality, from the tyranny of individuality and I can laugh till I fall down. No one holds me to then just drop me anymore. I made a decision, why should I walk out of my bedroom or into a workplace or into the day and take on someone else's mood or ideas or limits. Now I wear giant heels and crush the grasshoppers, all thoughts like popcorn popping around my head. I now say to myself why look at "the waves" (of insecurity, jealousy, fear, frustration). They will only sink you so now you know that, don't look at them as you get out that manky boat of limits. This is the time for vision. I do have the ability to see God's presence, his power, his plan in spite of the obstacles. Today is the day for living in vision. Am I cutting stones and they are just stones or do I see that I am building a great cathedral. Do I live despite the grey of the day? Each day can be a birth day.

Letter 36 (Making every day count)

Dear God, I decided today just how much persistence have we all got at the start of the day. We all have 24 hours. Who has pressed on through? Who has bothered to go with all their might into those precious hours and minutes: drill, to physically change something, to pick up and do? It is like wearing glasses. As it is no good trying to see without them because your vision will be blurred! This day is an opportunity, you want us to be blessed in our days, and can I see my day like that as clear as putting on glasses. Have I made my mind up yet so whatever comes at me, I am in focus. God wants us to have a fulfilled life, not a get out quick or get anything quick. God is a suddenly God, not a get it quick God. He may bestow things suddenly but they will be part of a God agenda. How much of what I do is me and how much is to save the Lord's shining reputation! Do I realise the effect of the sharpness of my faith in its fullest, like a sword in its sheath. I am fully protected yet am ablaze for truth! I cut through to the truth. I can cut. I can cut through the forest thicket of this world and go into the open fields of God's opportunities. Whatever, I wasted it is what I do now, not at what age I do it. Those years are gone. Do it right? I choose today when I will serve. My motive for today is Jesus. What am I allowing to rule me today? What good is prosperity, possessions and passion if it doesn't serve us and elevate Jesus! Do I tweak my priorities and rearrange them so I can be where I have been invited to be. Is God in the proper place, in the everything of my life? Is the balance in order? What dominates my life, my thoughts, my dreams, my ambitions, my finances, my time? God is my priority if he is not my number one, then it puts everyone else in the wrong place. Realign and resurrect and revive and renovate and refresh and rise up.

Letter 37 (Accepting constructive criticism)

Dear God, just thinking about accountability to be vulnerable and to let down my defensive walls, to be teachable and willing to learn, no matter how difficult the assignment and to be available to God and not caught up in the rush of life and to be honest to the truth, no matter how revealing. I am not alone in this vast life. I am not a random, vague dot of an island, hardly visible on a map of the world but I am part of a continent, a land of a body of beehives. It is so fantastic when another is on board with you on this land, who sees and loves you here, who sees the chaff and the grain and blows the rest away with a breath of kindness. Who makes you stop admiring the reflection of the moon in a lake but makes you look up and see the enormity of possibility in the sky as the real moon is shining down, and the real you is at last standing up. Not crouching over a reflection. Then I can raise my empty hands to God and find a fullness I never even knew existed. God can't pour into my hands if they are already full so I let go of the tight grip of fear and OCD. I don't forfeit my soul now. I don't need to piece myself with many griefs! No more leakage. I stand whole and clear and shiny like the moon and the visions can enlarge in my distress. I am stretched up into truth and life.

Letter 38 (Out the mould)

Dear God, I'm getting a backbone at last, escaping the mould of this world. Squeezing myself out of it and sanding down the surfaces of all the world's imprints! It is in my attitude today. Can I resist change, adaptation and alteration? Has the world grabbed me and stopped my blood supply so I don't know what the distinction is between custom and commandment. I can live in the spirit's freedom and freshness, not the human custom where it is all routines for show, just getting by. Legalism is so stuffed with its own self-righteousness it can't handle the festive freedom when it's time for merriment. Then I will celebrate, laugh, dance, and sing because the joy of the Lord is my strength. I don't need the freshness like freshly made wine, to pour out into old wine skins. God has stepped into my history and taken away my wrinkles. I don't want to be too brittle for freshness. I want it to soak in and make me burst with blossoms. Now I'm a Christian, God has made all things new. He wants my heart clean, cleaner than my hands. He wants my thoughts freshened by creativity and willing to take a risk. I will be in the God sounds, not the cracks of brittle twigs breaking, because now I want to bear fruit.

Letter 39 (Thank you for the dance)

Dear God, I finally climbed that last extra half mile up that unattractive little pathway, round the side of the plateau I've been on. And yep, I can see the view and yep, it is like a view I never knew could exist. It is in the steadfastness I'm learning, as now I have a reference point and by fixing my eyes on it, I regain my spiritual balance like a ballet dancer, spinning round, keeping one reference point. I realise just how important it is to ask for your favour, to be on me, to ask each day for your blessings and favour only in your favour, are the party lights switched on, what I mean is that surge of sudden feeling an exhilaration as I believe your favour is on me in that moment and you are smiling at me. I now can count my time in heart beats as I am excited about life again and I live in the pulse of life, a life really lived. It's like I've changed the record and found the tune and am in time with the rhythm of eternity. Finally, I am out of the potholes, no more sprained ankle of chaos. You see in secret, no one else can do that, so you know even before me where I'm at in my heart. So I clear my vision and blink and see. My heart fills with clear, warm drops of gratefulness. I open the eyes of my heart. Oh how you lavish me. I'm so grateful, Lord.

Letter 40 (A new shape)

Dear God, standing alone with you I know God plus one equals a majority! I can live away from the herd instinct, it's like shedding a skin and emerging from a cocoon. No more do I need to be deceived into staying a big lump of clay. I have thrown myself over moral cliffs. I don't need loss of standards anymore. That insecurity used to drive me into the "safety" of conformity. It's like I know you are putting me back on the potter's wheel and reshaping me. You alone can do that, taking me back and making me again. It really is amazing how gently and lovingly you have done this. I have been some odd shaped clay over the years and really messed up. Only you give meaning to my life my strength of character is not sapped and I don't need to cut off my branches. I used to be so self-destructive till I really learnt who you are. I only need to give the fruit away otherwise it will rot but no one has the right to take away my branches or cut them off. I can stand alone with you God in the way I think and be so much wiser in who I spend time with. I am of use to you again as I got up despite the choices I made you have no condemnation for me. You can still make something out of all my remnants. I am not so low anymore that I have to look up to see the bottom of the mess I was in. I know at any given time, I can choose to focus on my circumstances, others, myself or Jesus. I will stand and if it means standing in the gap, then that is what I will do. I stand up in my God given garments, my God shape and am ever so grateful.

Letter 41 (So grateful)

Dear God, I'm so grateful again and again that you came here to get me. You put your hands and feet and words in the wet cement of my life and made an imprint so deep and profound, it would forever mould my life. It doesn't matter how much wind and waves there are if you are in the boat with me. I can go out to the deeps where you surprise me, where I take you at your word and the mental nets of my life all broken and tangled up are untangled and I can throw the right untangled nets over the right side of the boat now! You have indeed calmed my storm. You have filled my nets because now I have thrown them on the other side. Now I live a life with respect and admiration. There is no blame or chaos surrounding it. My paths aren't crooked anymore. My feet don't rush into evil and there is no lack of discipline. Wisdom is my sister and I just don't stray off the path. I don't turn off into a cul-de-sac anymore as I know exactly the outcome. I know where my branches stretch out into and how ripe my fruit is. I stay on the road. I steer clear of the highway. The hook is taken out of my lower lip. God, you have melted all of me into shape. I am not unstable nor double minded in all I do. My light isn't hidden. I wear valuable jewels of my anointing. I am in my palace with my parade, which reflects in a pool back onto God's glory.

Letter 42 (Finally Home)

Dear God, so glad your dreams of me are now the life I'm living because I've finally, truly surrendered to you. That we have met in this place, over spiritual realities in a world that has stopped dreaming with you, I can dream. I can dare to dream because you do say in your word, just how much you have to give to those who ask. I don't need to fill the gaps anymore with stuff, as my background music is joy, to my everyday lifestyle, and I can go through the portal into another kind of life. I'm glad of the delicious stirring of hope I'm finally able to grasp hold of. There is a new ending out of a bad beginning. It is a wild hope I'm experiencing. I know now hope, instead of illusion. I stop nailing my old dreams onto my new faith. I have a Tupperware container of hope stored in my heart, like concentrated liquid, like orange juice and it multiplies with those I love and know. I am an adventure with you, Lord. This is an exciting journey. You are the hinge holding my life together and giving me whole, beautiful flexibility and I can step up into as you, of all people, don't limit me. I know you have reshaped me inside out, the swelling has gone down of pride and ego and now, oh, how I rest. Wow it's a great place to finally be.

Letter 43 (Thanking you for interrupting me)

Dear God, thank you. I don't let the lie inside the loss determine my future. That you have fixed me like a fixed jigsaw. That you interrupt me with one of your disturbing interruptions. I don't need to use my old ways of coping anymore. My secret bag of skills and aptitudes. I can let go and let you. I can now go to the place of risky newness and you step into my history and take away my wrinkles. I don't now feel that I am somebody if I get the smile, and nobody much when I'm on my own that is an emotional prison sentence. I am so relieved to dismantle the old ways of coping. You have exposed the lies that have ruled my life, yes I declare you have unearthed them! I am in the centre of your love. I think what we realised is the thing that I've been so trying to get rid of, is the actual crucible on which God chooses to shape my soul into something of beauty. It is the things you allow to remain, that are left there it seems to now serve your purpose in my life. It is like disturbing interruptions that transform me. I think once disillusionment strips me of illusions, you can finally give me what you had for me all along. It's great now I'm in that place because it's truly home. So if I veer away from it I feel and know that warning light. I now don't need to go away from my true home. I'm at home in my own skin. I am no longer in the illusion of control, illusion of low self-esteem, insecurity, jealousy, fear. Those were my own delusions. I don't leave my first love. Now I don't get seduced by a great variety of ways. Other voice will try to win the love I so much desire. I have woken up on the inside. To be relieved, cleansed, unburdened. I have found my heart and you have walked me into the embrace of love and kept my plate warm at your table. There is a place for me.

Letter 44 (The best is yet to come)

Dear God, it is as strange as sometimes the hardest time is when our dreams actually do come true! The humbleness I feel and the enormity of responsibility. To make sure my talents only take me where your character keeps me. I don't need to look in the rear-view mirror. I am being cut out into a new pattern. I don't add the regrets of the past to my fears of the future. I want to live this present moment. I want to rest in you so that when I get up, I am imprinted with you. So much is going on, on my behalf, I get to see peeks now and again but the whole working out of my life is up there in the universe and when I finally see the whole view, it will take my breath away. Oh what you do behind the scenes for my life, for you are writing a larger story than the one I can see. I am not at the whim of another person's choices or affections. You tie up all my loose ends into happier endings, past any horizon I can see! God is conducting an amazing orchestra and I'm listening to it through a crackly radio in the kitchen. Hearing the faint notes of God's song in my life. And life is mine to live and slowly but surely, the splinter is pulled out of my heart.

Letter 45 (How you look at me)

Dear God, your look of approval is everything to me and I don't need to tap into insecurities already roosting inside me. I am not paralysed by the power I give someone to name me. You have sprung the lock of the cage of disapproval and rejection as I hear your voice which is so much clearer and louder over everyone else's. I am pressed deeper into your heart, Lord. Those whose opinions hold too much power over me, I detach from. I listen through the noise. I hear you name me by name and that sticks to my ribs now. I do trust you Lord. In the places where old fears and insecurities controlled me, you enlarge the spaces in my cramped heart so even others can find refuge there. I can now see my shape as I become the shape you created me to be.

Letters 46 (Helping the broken-hearted and setting captives free)

Dear God, it is when my deep gladness and the world's deep hunger meet. I am now at the centre of who I am meant to be. What I have from you, Lord, to give to the world has come from my wounds and secret grief's. You were held on the cross, you couldn't move so that I can. I love the joy I feel when I am truly offering what I know I am meant to give. There is that strangely awful ordinariness that goes with any sort of gift or calling. I now have the courage to venture right into the middle of the actuality, not just getting my toes wet but full-on dive right in. I'm doing what you put right in front of me and trust you with the outcome. I'm so glad to be living out the small part of an extraordinary drama that is yours alone.

Letter 47 (Dancing today)

Dear God, I have finally got up to dance as my realest life has a chance to come true, like I've been rescued from the rubble of panic, terror and fear. So consumed yet still intact. I now know what is real and what I have wanted all along. I can live lavishly. It may seem scary to go out onto the dance floor of life, out of the comfort zone of habits. I find that all that I am is consumed in your love and only in you do I truly remain intact. You captured my heart in my chosen ache! I am led into places I never intended to visit. I want to be the proverbs woman in Proverbs 31, her strength and dignity are my clothing and I smile at the future. I will dance with the king one day so today I live in maximum love and happiness. I unwrap all the presents laid out for me. I am whole and new, free and happy. I don't now THINK 'Oh, is this it.' I think 'what's next!' and am amazed by my 'this is it.' I never need limit you again or live in limits of what dull lives dictate. It is so wonderful to be amazed by you.

Letter 48 (Defined by God)

Dear God, I'm 100 percent so sure of who I am now, in you. I need nothing more to define me. For you are my blueprint. I don't hide anymore but let you use me, all those things that make me, me! I won't be a people pleaser anymore. Neither will I be manipulated by family or friends.

I am not confused about my identity any more. So no one can now manipulate me. I know in you I am valued for how I am. And I can paint the world even more with my unique God colours. I feel I've broken out of a mould. I don't cast off restraint but keep focused. Jesus surrounded himself with different personalities. You encourage us all to be ourselves, to be in places and jobs that are not just the acceptable and limited suggestions of the world but that I can soar above all of that. Thank you for individual personalities. I'm not locked into anything today that would stop or limit my future. I am tuned into your frequency with my inner compass and heading in the right direction.

Letter 49 (On the stage of my life)

Dear God, this journey is quite amazing. I am standing on your toes like a little child dancing with their daddy, standing on his feet as he twirls them around. I am letting you lead. I hope I will follow and keep up as the dance has begun. I will keep up and learn the steps for the destination of who I was created to be so we are dancing into that life together. I feel like I am only seeing my lines for if this life were a script and God has got the whole play, he has the full script, he has cast me and the plot he devises. I now know my name. Of all the names given to me, over the years the ones you call me are the loudest, the clearest. I am finally in the play of my life and you are directing it. I have got scars and I do limp but it only reminds me of your goodness and what you have pulled me back from and how you place key people in my life, at just the right moments. I do have the right people walking with me even you, Jesus, turned to your disciples for guidance. I know I am fully myself, same as I have always been with a God side that can and does facilitate my God given dreams, ideas, and potentials. I know now why you made me the way you did. I rest assured as you know the beginning, middle and end of the acts of my life. Then there is the Holy Spirit. He is like the prompt at the side of the stage and I am at last, listening and picking up on my cues. I have altered my values and my identity isn't in labels, handed or imposed on me. Oh to be in grace, statute and wisdom. You see past all my excuses and all I've done which made my journey longer. I kept going the wrong way. What could have taken a year has taken over 30. I am glad to finally be on the right stage in the right play written by you. I don't curl up in the armchair of my life anymore. I get up and at it, I separate myself and let you lead me out and up and into the spotlight.

Letter 50 (Right friendships)

Dear God, I know my name in you and the name you called my life breath into being. Thank you for the right people on this journey with me. We all express and excel at being realest us, which brings a combination of results and satisfaction. All my relationships are in my life by choice, not by accident or default. They all help me grow even more into who I truly am. They are also the realest I've ever met and known. I don't need the insecurities in my heart when I am with them for they do not betray me. With a secure heart, it enables me to take giant leaps in the direction I am travelling. I am not competing but each of us lets our life gifts and callings complement each other. I live a stable life, not with stabilisers on. I am not unstable anymore with changeable emotions and inconsistent reactions to situations. I don't have people that confuse me anymore, for insecure people will make me lose my momentum. Rather, friends bring empowerment and release and encourage my dreams and aren't threatened by the real me or try to control me. I do not go into misguided detours from my intended route anymore.

Letter 51 (Lies are unearthed)

Dear God, my journey is so much fun now Lord. It's used to be an endurance test but I have invested in a memory bank of vital information. So my internal alarm goes off. I will not be hijacked again, no more people looking for a point of weakness in me and striking when I'm most vulnerable. No more being infiltrated through the doorway of compromise. My defence now is remembrance! I have programmed my memory and stored experiences so I remind myself with key calendar dates. Just how good my God is to me and all he has done! I have a flint, face forward and not distracted. Feelings are very persuasive and I need to control their power. A zone is entered. I am a Christian, I am in God's zone and finally stick to the speed limit. It's for the best. I refuse to spend my life being manipulated by my feelings or the feelings of others. I don't slow down anymore, to pick up unwanted hitchhikers who tell me that religion is a waste of time and fill my car journey with their fumes. My conviction takes me past the negative report and perspective others have of the situation they believe I am in. I started with a desire, a dream that compelled me to take a step. I HAVE STOOD UP INSIDE.

Letter 52 (To have right relationships)

Dear God, May I be rightly related to you of all the relationships I face in the day. I need to be aware of the subtle adaptations and conscious compromises. I'm so glad that in my relationship with you, I am truly free as all my thoughts and feelings are revealed. Because of my wholeness with you, Lord, my spirit I feel is awakened and my spirit interacts in my life with others. The vibes are then right as we are on each other's wavelength and "click". I can be real and draw others out to be real also. Likewise, with you Lord, you demand you can do no more with me and take me no further till I improve my personal relationship with you. I know in the right relationship, I can combine my efforts and resources and do and accomplish what I couldn't on my own. It is so great to have a goal, a meaning/vision, and a goal in sight. I know with you as my vision, the rest of my relationships can fall into their natural state and place in my life! I know that intimacy produces vulnerability and it requires commitment, for its security to be felt. I have learned where privacy is respected, real intimacy can flourish. I'm glad of communication even when there are different perspectives. I never put my assumptions up for discussion that can cause the other person to be defensive and irritated and resentful! I'm glad to face relationships now, and let love, trust, respect and understanding grow. By loving you, Lord, my need for divine unchanging love is satisfied and now I can receive and give up and down variable love away all over the place, warm passionate, friendly affectionate caring as the spirit work and I can work it out in proper human love and responses.

Letter 53 (True friendships)

Dear God, I don't need my divine love from any human. I now know of gentleness and it cannot flow from weakness but only as its roots are in your strength so it is protective and reassuring and makes the person receiving it feel secure and cherished. I am so glad I am around others that actually speak out love. I now build trust, not test its limits. So I don't stretch mine or another's capacity too far, too fast. I know a character is shown up in its truest light in a crisis. Fear has led to anger as anger is an emergency emotion. Thank you, you value me as a person. May I be the one that gives honour and respect to another's spirit? To be around someone who wants to understand me immediately, releases me from the need to justify my behaviour or opinions. Someone who manipulates and dominates me, that person is dishonouring. I enter another frame of reference with intention and attention. I stand in their shoes and see through their eyes. If I can establish and maintain relationships at the level of the spirit than that will make light work of the complexities of communication and I can unscramble messages. My spirit does not live in the cramped attitudes of meanness of spirit. No more irrational or emotional agendas. No more pettiness. My energy is not taken anymore! You heal and restore my body to a right relationship with its environment. I adjust to and harmonies my acts and attitudes with others and use internal energies, such as anger, in the correct way to face life. Thank you.

Letter 54 (Right Love)

Dear God, if love becomes our God it destroys us in emotions that can turn to hate. We are all broken in part and ask for too much attention from others which they in turn haven't got to give you are the scale I measure myself by. I am glad I am weighed by the angels. Oh to sit on a mountain and see the city. You give me noble love, Lord. I come home to you are the God shape of love my soul rests in. I hope I'm not too far away from the city but I am near those that need you. I can go into that city cook them a meal, take them out and enjoy fellowship. I don't need to live by pleasures that gratify my senses but pleasures of appreciation that fully deserve my attention and deserve to be enjoyed. You want us to have fun. I know of sensual and aesthetic love as I see the pleasure of the Garden flowers and yet then also have the enjoyment of its beauty. I experience "need love", "appreciate love", and "gift love". I am learning to get to know a person's character after initially loving their personality. May I practice more and more domestic courtesy in my life? May my imagination not exceed my obedience so I imagine I am tasting of love? I do love, truly, I do. "Affection" produces happiness only if there is give and take and common sense and decency. You need to add reason to affection and justice and you need goodness and humility for affection to be honourable. Friendship makes me ask, do we care about the same truth. We may not agree on the answer but if we both care about the little question that is of importance to me. Oh to see the tragic comedy of life and the pathos too, so two people click. To meet on such an internal level is safe. Help me to know the right love. The Eros love a passionate romantic love. The philia love of friendship and the agape love that is selfless. I could give pleasure which would push me to the extreme and it will shatter us in pain. Oh the grandeur and terror or love and all its playfulness. Oh to liberate the splendour. In you God, I am the flute, you are the notes of my life.

Letter 55 (Going deeper)

Dear God, thank you that I can stop the rush of the impetuous decision based on imaginative emotions. That I can stay in the right stance, attitude, perception, and disposition.

You have led me back to grace and refined my mind and with you, my soul finds its truest fulfilment. I know that this depth is what happens when I find you. I don't want to dress you in a cheap suit anymore and live uncomfortable for the rest of my life. I know how to use my talents and it is a great responsibility in this day of reckoning. You hide the vastness of yourself in the deepest dimensions of my inner existence. Deep is your dwelling place, Oh God. Deep is indeed the gift of discipline. I go deep, not to get more intellectual but I go deep to taste your reality. When I pray that is my portal into your deep. I don't want to fill my life with the same old appetite but stretch myself, try new recipes and expand my horizon. I reach for you in love and you reach back into my deep, in the centre of my existence where no eye has seen, no ear has heard, no mind can realise the love and what you have for me. May I be disciplined? May I be immovable, using my breaks, not to be quiet but discern things, be true? I use my steering wheel. May I get a heavenly perspective on all my real values? It is what I take up that catches heaven's esteem. May I wait for you to fill the vacuum and not let consuming appetites swarm through my better intentions? I hunger after what you want, rather than merely quoting what you don't want for me. May I not lose vision because of neglect? I have caught sight of the significance of my worth by God and myself. I spend myself and wait and weep.

Letter 56 (Right identity)

So I hide heaven's treasures in my inward life. A displacement takes place for my appetite is now to be all for you. I used to crave getting things needing things. I make holy the days of my life. I do not need to rush. I am at one with you. I do not have a past only a future. I am hungry for a relationship with you Lord. Like being with a good friend through all the chatting just sitting in the pleasure of each other company. The wonder of togetherness with you is all I desire. I hold on to decisions until I hear from you for it is your destiny that I crave. I use my time now to magnify you not exalt myself. May I not flee in disorder from victory already won. I live in overwhelming awe? May desperations of life not prevent me from enjoying you? The stories I tell locate us all in our human condition with our eyes looking to heaven. I will not make Christ in my image but be confirmed by the renewing of my mind. I write with ordinary ink of the absolute greatness of our God. I want to cry out how beautiful you are and give you my all. You are forever beautiful and when I praise you it is with my whole heart and leaves me weak so I can be of use for you and your kingdom.

Letter 57 (Burn my lips)

Dear God, I burn in your love. I ask is this worthy of love and celebrate my security by my prayers. I lie my ego down. It only craves health and wealth. I want to be worthy of love in this fragile world. I want you to impact me so profoundly that all my wants are changed from material to eternal. I want my heart to run ahead of itself with joy. I want to be the mature in my spirituality where I arrive at a sense of abundance that isn't related to the material and I am content as you are, in the process of finishing us and I can renounce the bustle. My heart can resonate with delight for you have found me, Lord. I want to be transformed by the nature of the light that is in me. I live out the agony and the ecstasy, the elation and terror and I seek and find you. I don't want my mind to be numb. I want to engage with your word. I wish people would quit making God seem dull. The consuming fire has been domesticated into a candle flame. I move inside my inner life. I don't want to sit on my hands but I want to act, to do. I don't want to live in such shallow soil that thrives my ego and doesn't give roots to any of God's purposes. I can be fully self and in you, Lord, and with your glory coming into my fragile, finite life. I draw and listen to you, Lord, listening is centering too. I hope my inwardness becomes too small to hold your immensity. I experience the hush of truth. I don't want to be tied to dust anymore and I scorn dust and fly.

Letter 58 (Live out your calling)

Dear God, thank you for showing me life in the spirit where two roads converge and are mystery and passion. I know you wait for those who love you and for those that hunger for things too excellent to be understood. I hang your picture in my gallery and stand in your warm reality. You will watch over me, you search the whole earth for those whose hearts are longing to know you. I have learnt Christ at last. Oh, if only we could get such mystery, awe and wonder back into the church. No more the dullness of business as usual! Let the churches not substitute hype for fire. Oh God be the noises in our homes and churches. I don't want to be a Christian that smiles and shakes hands and stays away from the core of the pain in others. We go to church in straw hats. We should be wearing life saving equipment. For God will wake up and truly take offense. You met with those that actually needed a physician, I want to go to church and meet the needs of others. Do I live fully in the mystery of Godliness? The mystery of things too excellent to understand or will my worship just l reflect empty worship. Oh that I will learn to do your work I want to heal the broken hearted and set the captives free for I know what it is like to walk around covered in shame and chains. I know the glory of divine mayhem that comes in the visitation of God as it is not always orderly. I seek you in the ordinary ways and the things that have too much excellence for me. I am a prisoner of the only reality that there is. I have been torn from the clutches of this world. Oh we live the longest if we know we are alive in the first place. I do have a real reason to be in this world. There is a holy fire shut up in my bones that can be of use for your glory. I can win big games when I learn to play with the little hurts of life. Oh that I am chosen, a chosen person in the furnace of humiliation. I have been there and you were there with me and now I am out of it. You do sometimes heal by breaking. We take it till we make it. My call keeps me telling the truth. I have been made rich with wounds that only you can heal. I treasure the pain that sculpts me.

Letter 59 (Please carve me into my God shape)

Dear God, my adventure is you. Like an artist, you look at the stone and see the image. May I yield in head, heart, knee, tongue? Does my heart even understand what I am saying! Where my knee bends, my character is born. I don't want to sip on you, Lord, I want to take huge gulps. If I live as if I have no knees, my life has no centre and no end. Until I lose control, do I see your character come through in me, in discipline and work? Personality is cheap but character is not for sale. By not craving God, I keep the best of life at arm's length. Oh, I have lived in that haunting loneliness. Do I hear your breathing on the cross when your character bled on the word? Did I see what truths are true! May I not have loss of balance in my basic being? May my habit of my soul rest in you. I don't want to keep stumbling over the same stone. I am being used past my healed brokenness.

Letter 60 (Facing fears)

Dear God, yes life is your Joy not the world's happiness as that like a new-born baby always needs feeding. Your Joy is completely different if we would only seek for it more people would see Christ in us. The Joy of the Lord is my strength. My elation conversion is permanent and I can sing, even in the grey days I can celebrate as I am restored. I realise what that means now. I have finally bought the truth and I will never sell it again. The truth has set me free. My terror lies between confidence and low self-esteem. I now dare myself to believe I am OK. I have the courage to face my fears without blinking both those surprise fears and the ongoing fears. I feel powerless to put the pieces of my life back together sometimes but burnout is not the final state, rather confession makes God my partner. By facing my fears, stepping out into the fear like a bird out of the nest I can see fear is an illusion that needs to be tamed. Confession is the birth canal of courage. It heals my fears. I can face the valley of the shadow of death without despair. Guilt will not conquer me. Confession causes me to lay down my burdens and stand free. Phew! I live now what matters most. Through the fires and the sorrows, I want to preserve the self-God created me to be.

Letter 61 (where I place my confidence)

Dear God, thank you for the new laws of life in us. The appreciation of the life that is ours. I will not let my current circumstances control my mood. I celebrate the moment. This is the day the Lord has made I will rejoice and be glad in it. You have cut me to the quick, Lord, and heal the diseases of my soul. I will not join the dark side of my personality and fall into despair. I gain true humility, not by putting myself down but by standing next to Christ I declare, 'With God I can.' Comparison only leads to discontentment and separation. Satan is defeated by the absence of any pride in me. I have understood so little of what is around me as I haven't used what is within me! Like the grass and flowers, may I grow in deep silence and like the sun and moon, may I move in silence. When I become discouraged, I can look up. I have changed residences. I traded in clay for gold, protoplasm for spirit, the temporary for the immortal. I move into the depths of God and your treasure house. I sit at your table home at last. Out of the desert at last.

Letter 62 (Coming home)

Dear God, hurrah. I knew my way home! Sometimes my security trembles before my own disbelief. I needed to unlearn so much; nothing is more certain than God's predictability. I exist to get ready to meet God. I live in a vibrant faith as I step out of my secular life. Heaven is a place where I am home with you and I will know what now here on earth makes me tremble. The absolute amazing awesome incredible overwhelming home that I will live in forever with you. Obedience has made me supple. I do not need brittle fear anymore. You have assembled the odd pieces of my life, and I can ask what daring things do I have the courage to do? You are a God of the impossible. In the deep, I find you. So I come out of the desert and I am glad of all the suffering in the dry barren desert. How the experiences of humiliation, shame, terror horrors have formed me and made me all that God intended. God has meant it for good. I never take anything for granted again, I am so deeply grateful that you found me and I wash it all away in your river of life that runs from under your throne. Heavens waters have come and run through my desert bringing me a life worth living. I can now live out the wonder of it all! Thank you for being the river in my desert.

Chapter 2
Sentences

A struggle of mine has been to change thought patterns, to erase the black thoughts wherever they came from it could be something spoken over me as a child or people I have let influence me, I was so naïve and trusted so readily believing what people said. It is not till you try to break these thought patterns that you realise how the roots go so deep. Yet we all struggle on some level with doubts and fears in the middle of a crazy, disappointing day. We put on an air of confidence but that little three years old lost in the supermarket "feeling" is there lurking as life is so fragile. I think if we can carry a sentence with us each day from the word of God, his living word can feed our souls, his power can erase the devils lies. I have realised how much power the word of God has. As an actress learns her lines and makes it real, so we have been given the power of imagination to live a freedom frowned on by a broken world. So these sentences can be spoken out in your mind in the middle of that rush hour Tube journey, and in the middle of some meeting that has become monotonous, and they can be a reminder of the fresh faith you live by and the point of your existence… I call it the FIRM HOPE CLOTHES LINE…PIN EM ON!!!

Once you change your mind, all that is right will follow. I renew my mind.

I let go of others limits and fears over my life. I have a Caleb attitude.

I have turned the corner back into my calling.

God takes me seriously and I'm allowed to be me. He does accept me. I am the apple of his eye.

I realise – in the Lord, not in the problem.

I claim your prayers in Gethsemane. I can overcome the pain of memories.

I identify with the Holy Spirit's beauty, not the weight of low self-esteem.

I accept changes. I do not need to live in fear.

I am a steward of my body, mind, work and money.

Perseverance in this builds my character for the next goal in my life.

I feel upside down, but I am the right way up.

You are holding onto my right hand. I am lifted up.

This present moment is a firm vision and firm hope I can break out-of-date habits.

I dismount the tiger. No bears or lions, pigs or foxes catch me.

I'm getting rid of things all the time no more easily besetting sin.

The light is on so the shadows, have to flee.

I passed the exam. I don't need to re-sit. I am more than a conqueror.

I don't live other's visions, I will go from pit to palace like Joseph.

Melt me refiner's fire in the mould and fill me and use me. Gold through furnace.

I know who I am without that addiction in my life. I don't have a past only a future.

I am sanctified and can claim calmness, order and sanity in this moment.

I know my "bent" (my inner soul is in balance with my outer personality), only in you Lord.

God has overloaded me with hope.

I'm free to fly as I understand the way behind the fear.

I find relief from needless guilt. You broke the power of cancelled sin.

My man-made Goliath is too big to miss.

The narrowest hinge in my hand puts to scorn all machinery.

What I let go and surrender then those gaps and pauses can be God filled with the Holy Spirit.

I'm in the vice grip of God, not fear.

Happiness comes by seeing God's perception.

I leave it at the cross. It is out of date and rotting. Don't pick up the stink.

I love God's standards. I take the best, the bread not the stones.

I step out in victory as I'm in the spirit of love, power and self-discipline.

I am an ewe-lamb.

I force my will to believe. Help my unbelief.

My life is hid with Christ. Yes I'm safe as the devil can't get in. He can't find me.

I'm on the bridge and it is fixed. I can go to the other side.

I do not need to live life cycles of the past.

I chat to you on the shore and as the dawn rises.

I meet you in the "library" of your word in the evening.

I have the courage to live this risen life.

Good morning, Lord. I invite you. Please take all my unconfessed sins.

I seek you first in this day. Have I recognised you yet today?

You hold my mind. Problems exist when I doubt you.

I live today in moments.

I do the best in all I do.

The light leads me so I live in it, not the shadows around.

My dream is real.

I stay amazed at your awesomeness.

I live in your framework today and paint with your colours.

Help me to keep up the eagerness so what I hope for comes true.

I run in such a way so as to win the prize.

Please keep my mind open to the hope.

The past is gone so no more self-inflicted mustard-gas invisible thoughts.

I let it go. The battle belongs to you.

I will resist the devil and he will flee.
I live won.
I live the facts, not the feelings.
I walk in your strength alone and a spirit filled life only.
You are the notes and I am the flute. I sing Intune
I am intimate with you I am known by you.

I live already won as you only died once, it is finished. I don't have a past only a future.

I open the gifts on my bed all the presents you leave me each morning as I wake.

I am your beauty. Beauty for ashes.

I let shadows go, they have no power.

I release my fear of the new and with open hands and open heart, hold on to you.

I live doing, not mulling. I get up and go.

Take my guilt, my low self-esteem. Make me whole.

You're holding me and I let go so both my hands are in yours.

I don't live neurotically. I am whole set free in newness of life.

Help me not to have my hands too full of stuff so they can carry and do what you ask.

I don't let old patterns in.

Thank you for showing me that I can live, not just exist

Like Jonah, I have turned around.

The dove has returned. I now know the things that belong to my peace.

I tattoo your word on my heart each day.

I am that five-year-old girl in Cyprus walking through the vine hearing you

Gold seeds of truth are sewn into my heart.

I live Ark-shut led decisions

I am back to my first love.

I choose this day whom I will serve.

God, do my life, my first love lives with me. He is my partner.

I erase black thoughts.

I am now desperate for my first love.

I run when temptation comes near like Joseph did.

I don't fight against the Goads.

It is over so let go the best is real.

I am careful not to quench the Holy Spirit.

Am re-clothed in a cloak the cross wove into the thread.

Behind the doing is the power of the reality of God. So pour and the glass comes.

Take the weeds and thorns out of my mind and life.

I am an oak, not a reed. I have cedar root strength

Jesus has opened my grave and I see what I am without him.

My dry bones can live.

I am hinges of perfume clay shaped in holiness.

Habits go – way of life come.

The nightmare is over.

Thank-you Lord, you are my first love.

I love you enough to stop sinning. The strain brings enough regret to change.

Rush is wrong. I stay calm and rest in the cleft. I am no more in impulses so out of control in urges, I do not live in panic terror.

I am in strong, calm sanity. I have lifted my eyes to heaven and my understanding has returned to me.

Oh Lord, help me obey you so that I am pressed into the consequences of obedience.

I am abandoned to the love of Christ.

Thank-you Lord, you are in the common place things and people around us. I do the duty that lies nearest.

Intensely narrow my interests on Earth and immensely broaden my interest in God.

I deliberately turn my imagination to God.

Now I hear you. It is such a delight. My shame is in having been so long in hearing you.

Arise and eat and do the next thing. Irreparable becomes the irresistible future.

Thank you for the miracle of yesterday that encourages me to step even further into faith.

Help my personal holiness turn into abandonment to God so I can do, not think: "am I of use but rather am of value to the living God."

I am spent for you.

Help me believe in your finite power apart from my finite understanding of it.

Help me to draw from the depths of the wells in me.

I will not counterfeit the love of God by working along the line of the natural, human sympathy.

You have plugged me in. I am plugged into joy, the fulfilment for which I was created and regenerated.

Nothing can wedge in between God and me.

I live a life uncrushed as I look to God.

I let go of solid sins. I lay hold of righteousness.

I am certain that I know I do not know. That is my secret of going with Jesus.

The devil can't find my mind. I am in the cleft.

I don't let any dispositions rule me. I am not blinded to the things which belong to my peace.

My faith is worked out in actualities. I do possess spiritual grit.

Thank-you Gethsemane. You feared you might not get through as the son of man, you knew you'd get through as the son of God but you did.

I can crash on the heartbeat of God.

I decide definitely about sin.

Each strand of sin goes so God can clothe me in his righteousness.

I kick it off my heel for in my weakness, I am strong.

I have passions, not addictions.

I have bread, not stones.

I keep myself exercised and fully fit, in God.

I learn to live in the grey days according to my mountain top experiences.

I burn my bridges and stand committed.

I never revise my decisions and make sure I make them in light of the high hour.

I hold on to what I know so no one takes my crown.

I live out the inspiration of my vision.

I step into my new nature, a whole makeover.

I rely on facts, not feelings. You died and rose again.

I yield to you Lord. Not to that old disposition.

I don't sew into the flesh in which I have no confidence and which, through corruption causes, consequences that are limited by the world and end in destruction.

I stop using fabulous, joy, and beauty in all the wrong areas.

I live a single heart purpose, not a double mind as it is over and once over, do it. So think no more on it (moronic)!

The matinee is over, the habits were the matinee film rewinding. False walls are down.

My jigsaw is fixed all the pieces have been found.

I am a disciplined warrior, fully prepared.

I account for all the bricks I am building with.

He is there all the time. I never knew it.

My moments of inspiration are my standard and my standard is my duty. I am never in danger of being led away by such moments.

I don't just have what I have experienced but the "more than" in the actual inspiration of the vision of God.

Because of Jesus' identification with sin, I have to radically alter all my sympathies and I substitute God's interest in others instead of my natural sympathy with them.

I bow my neck to his yoke alone and I never bind a yoke on others, not placed there by Jesus.

Is there a freshness and an energy in my day to day attitude as my horizon is the vision of God?

The good is always the enemy of the best.

You Lord, show me what I am without you.

I do not think about self-pity. It is the pride, rather, just get on with my Jesus errands.

I am consistent to God. I am stamped with moral spontaneous originality. I am blasted out of my prejudices into devotion to Christ.

Take the risk – don't be ignorant. Don't wait for intellectual understanding but just go. It truly is "pour and the glass comes".

Unlearn = yes! Make sure your relationship with God is as simple as it has ever been. Unlearn the "somethings" in your life!

I am out of the tree I come down and meet the Jesus who loves me so much and accepts me as I am.

I live the spirit of love, power, self-discipline and a sound mind.

I erase black thoughts = I am grown up. I do not need to be in a blind panic. I am in control of myself.

I have awoken from a nightmare and I am truly home. I am out of dark corners and lost maps and directions that end in dead ends.

I am in my bent, as God made me. The episodes, the cycles are indeed over!

To choose to suffer is wrong but to choose God's will, even if it means suffering, is a very different thing.

I hold a diamond in my hand.

I obey God's chastising, not self-delusions made by the devil.

I do not need to pick up that thing again.

I am not blind on this point anymore. I am not where I thought I was.

I let God grip me by his power and get me into attitude of mind and spirit, so I am at any cost, sanctified wholly.

I need not sin.

I am a sharp shooter. I get the devil smack between the eyes.

The disease leaves as God is an "at once" God.

God has broken the power of cancelled sin.

Be in the habit of having no habits.

Thank you. You have given me back the years the locusts have eaten.

My mind is safe. You have made the crooked paths straight.

No more self-pity for I am restfully certain that God answers prayer. Self-conscious awakens self-pity. I am not consciously conscious as only a sick person knows what health is. God has indeed established rest.

May every public thing be stamped with the presence of God?

Thank you. That prayer has worked wonders in my disposition.

I respond don't react to my life in the circumstances around me, in the context of fulfilling God's purpose and keeping in the light as God is in the light.

Thank you. No thoughts bind me. I am free. Thoughts are gossamer threads and not chains. I break them as I am hid with Christ.

Oh may I be holy in walk, thought and talk and manifest what God has given me.

May I pour my blessings out as sweet waters so that others would get their horizons enlarged through me?

I live passions, not addictions.

I come back to my right sense and stop my sinful ways.

I receive freely, not needy, you always give more than enough, I can come back for seconds.

At the turning point, I lean into you.

I forget the thoughts as they attack.

No to habits, I let go and the real life can come.

I got the stains of the world out.

Sin starts to grow in the mind.

I don't resist (like an exam). I have everything appertaining to my life.

I live in the shadow of the cross, not the shadow of fear.

I am not walking on broken glass anymore.

Lines have fallen for me in pleasant places.

I don't let invisible gas thoughts in.

I have the same power that raised Jesus from the dead.

Beware, lest I forget God's purpose for my life.

I don't mix up my own ingredients into the workings of my soul.

God has put me in the very nature of God.

God has attached my conscious life and all the deeper regions that I could not get at, into harmony.

I believe in who I am in God, not in my temperament, despite the chaos, I am the Lord's.

Lord, your name is closer than any thoughts.

I am dragged into the light and seen what the darkness is now!

I get into God's stride, walking on straight paths. I am out the cul-de-sac.

I walk through the corridor of my life, I see what God has framed as me.

My hands stay on the plough.

I walk this way, opening and seeing through the curtain.

I am the realest me.

I buy the field now. Your treasure is there for me.

Plans, like prophecies, laid out like a fleece – to come true.

I can be exceptional in the ordinary things.

I train my impulses into intuition by discipline.

Help me walk on dry land with you and not wander off.

Old things are passed away.

I step over the rocks of my life into real faith.

Like Jesus, I let mistakes correct themselves.

I don't need to follow my horoscopes as wherever God's will is in ascendant, all compulsions are gone.

Jesus will tax the remotest star and the last grain of sand to assist us.

Health is having sufficient vitality on the inside against things on the outside.

Holiness is the balance between my dispositions and the law of God expressed in Jesus Christ.

My I live my new life in conscious repentance and unconscious holiness, never the other way around.

Remorse at having made blunders is just disgust with myself. Instead, may I repent and say I have indeed sinned.

I give up the right to myself.

It is the right, noble and good from the natural standpoint that keeps up from God's best.

God searches the whole earth to find me.

Hesed love means I don't need to be afraid anymore.

Thank you. You love me like Hosea loved Gomer (Hosea 2 v14)

I am marvellously helped.

My soul is not patched up is woven in a new shape with the life thread of God.

I wrestle all to lay hold of the strength of God. I will not let go until you bless me.

Faith is doing, despite the illogical. Step out on the water, I do not look at the waves.

The weight of truth is weighted in prayers.

I have turned around and found the path of freedom.

I do not need to go out impetuously. God is my reward.

God reaches into the past and makes a house clearance. He sweeps up and finds my shekel.

No hurry of impetuous delight, nor the flights of impulse thoughtlessness.

Yesterday is irreparable but my God transforms destructive anxiety into constructive thoughtfulness.

I sleep on the bosom of Jesus.

I leave carrier bags of despair and shame at the cross and throw waste into the sea of forgiveness.

Don't trip on something behind you.

I am now my blueprint and I live in the whole mapped out areas. I do not waver off the map any more.

No to catastrophic thinking. The devil can't find my mind. It is hid.

The cross is erected in front of my vision.

I hold onto God now, not fear or low esteem.

God has changed his mind about me.

Remove the limits and transform the circumstances.

I stay in the place of beholding despite my day, the cross is empty!

I am gold through furnace for in the pressure of the furnace room, God is found.

God has broken into my life.

Lord, cement up the past.

Lord, you touch and we fall backwards.

To see reality in and via a spiritual dimension.

I lay the tracks of my life not wasted now for the same power that raised Jesus from the dead electrifies my tracks.

You came back for me Lord.

Alone with Jesus, all noisy questions have gone.

My God shape is filled no more wrong shape.

God haltered my life to rebalance, recharge and it is alive now.

I am at the end of self and of value to God.

I leave the irreparable.

God only answers the door to the best!

I don't put the Ark (God's majesty) in a man-made box!

Despite natural temperament, complete in Christ released from the chaos of ego.

I don't need to bruise myself on the stones of the past.

I can lose the unnecessary weight from my heart.

I venture out of whirlwind, grasping the crumpled vision. Jesus will iron it out.

Habits go, way of life comes.

Go deep with Jesus. Don't stay on the surface.

I lay it on the altar. I trust God like Abraham did.

I am safe in the middle of God's will it is the safest place to be.

I am an amateur at handling hope.

I walk on God's foundation.

I don't need to re-sit my past. It dissolves.

Devil – take your hand off me!

My land is fenced in – no more lumbering wagons of regret, my seeds can grow and change the landscape.

I live on the other side of my feelings.

I stay in the secret place behind the words and circumstances of my heart in God's hidden place.

My soul waits silently for you, Lord.

I enjoy the journey and I manage the success as I value the vision of my spirit.

Line my life up with your words.

I have got my stuff back. There is a line in the sand. My sand has shifted permanently.

God's drawings are always bigger, I do not limit him.

I leave the spirit of control and let go of being self-destructive.

No more living! It is over.

I have crossed the road and can get on the bus of second chances.

I am wrist free of wild, irrational sin.

Whole circle safety. May I live in the centre of your will?

All gifts come from the same place as the Holy Spirit. I don't need to look anywhere else!

I live the inspiration of my vision.

My nets are mended and fixed. I pull them untangled from the right side of the net.

I come back into the light, away from perplexities, you are not a God of confusion.

Oh, the intimacy with the Almighty.

I remind my heart where it belongs.

My I be spared from, to become.

My happiness is not based on happenings.

I turn up to the awakening of my life.

I am the right state on the inside.

I crash into God's heartbeat.

I am stamped with holiness.

I am out of the fiercest gales.

I realise that across the ages and years, prayers are for me! Renew my days of old.

I protect the temper of my mind.

I wear the mantle of safety.

God's will is an ascendant, all compulsion is gone.

God will use even the remotest star and the last grain of sand to help us.

I am marvellously helped, the spiritual has overtaken the natural.

I have expressions to the truth that struggled for utterance in me.

I sow the seeds, not the fruit. I use the fruit to bless others.

God picks me up and I have a better view of my life.

I look into the right places now.

The world's truth is a flickering candle compared to the bright sun of the Son of God!

Heal my nerves, Oh Lord.

Help me see the God that I have missed and cast away.

I have run far enough to realise I have a second chance and start with all I have not actually started.

I am free as God is bigger than any problems that loom or obstacles or persons.

I take God out of the box of my limitations.

Faith breaks through to dependence.

I can walk, not faint, in the ordinary.

I dust off my gifts – I am out of the cul-de-sac.

I belong to my peace.

I crash into God's heartbeat!

The truest me is not in these habits.

I gently step over so simply, so gently.

I let go of useless anxiety!

I stay in multiplications of love, planned over the years. It is worked out.

No more sand in my shoes. Shake it out.

I fear less and love more.

Jesus fills in my outline, my sketch becomes a picture.

I find the tune and I am in tune so I dance.

This is my acceptable year. The year of the lord's favour.

Take the miracle, not the way out, or you will end up way out!

I am made right inside out.

In you alone, I am extraordinary.

We look for a corpse but hear the risen voice.

I live out the right handbag!

Every new day feel the zap freshness of God's touch.

I can't build a fire with ashes. It is finished.

All my weeds have turned to cornflowers.

You have stepped into my history and taken away my wrinkles.

I am back into my vision stride.

I adjust the inequality and pull out the strands of lies from my mind.

Worry is interest you pay on borrowed trouble.

I gather what I did. Despite it being scattered by deceitful people.

He calls me, not screeches. His noise is the right level of noise.

I am hot, not lukewarm.

Ark shut decision.

Been in a hole, now I'm whole.

40 days after Easter Jesus went home. I am kept.

I am not dictated to by lies as I walk down the corridor seeing pictures of my past.

I go the narrow way.

I don't look back. I say no to the rear-view windows.

Life has taken root in me.

Cross of Christ strikes and impacts the roots.

I let go of scorpions and fires in my lap.

Pruned, I stop at once.

I reclaim my dream.

God broke the power of cancelled sin.

The giants are too big to miss.

My heart washes truth up.

God will, in no wise, fail me.

I have peace on all sides.

I have got the same power that raised Jesus from the dead.

Nightmare is over. I'm awake.

I work from the centre of God's will.

I rearrange my mental furniture around you Lord.

Clear the silt out of the stream. Declutter my mind.

Oh may I not go back to where I was, when you want me to be someone I've never been.

I marry my gifts with God's call.

I enter the zone in which I was made to live.

I dance into your favour.

I'm strong enough to take it off.

The weeds and thorns go and seeds can now breathe and blossom.

I don't look at the waves I step out immediately.

My heart is ablaze.

I turn around into my best days.
Your own hand put me in the cleft.
You put my heart back in and turned it on.
I am set free from the worthless manner of life, handed down by my ancestors.
Don't waste life by looking at a flea on the foot of an angel who happens to be dancing on the head of a pin.
I drop the habits. Grips go!
I laugh the days into colour.
The "x" is God so rest as He is the equation.
I am my vision shape.
Ignore thoughts, they will dry up like leaves and blast out of the Garden.
Nothing need terrify me.
It is time for a complete change of mind.
I cannot be shaken. I stand in awe on solid foundations.
I am driven by love, not fear.
Live by the rules of the vision.
I will not be mastered by anything.
God can start a new chapter, a new book with me at the start.
Take care of things on loan: body, money, family, work!
Your thoughts shape your future.
I am the new start of the plan for my life.
I can rest as he cried in Gethsemane.
The Lord in me is not imitation.
I live my individual Bent.
Life loses its drudgery and fear when you're in an act of worship.
Be as liberal now as you were in your sinful nature! Reckless for God instead.
God grows above so those who pray, horizons must ascend.
Let go of damp stagnant stench with a soulful face!
God takes all the horror off the walls of the corridor of my life.
I have unlearnt my yesterdays.
Lines have fallen for me in pleasant places.

Don't let my humanness hold me back with the nowhere people.

The past is only shadows.

God moves the boulder. All we have to do is believe.

I call for back up!

I step out of the shadows of memories.

Emancipated out into personality.

My faith has made me well.

Hurt to death (all old me!)

Don't let trivial keep me from doing and completing the task.

I am loved back to where I am meant to be.

Gods' riches at Christ's expense.

Can't train the heart like we train an animal. The tongue reveals the heart.

Obey God in haphazard things and through these pinholes, see the face of God.

We are a bundle of possibilities let god untangle the nets.

If you stand for everything, you fall for anything.

God corrects us. He takes us out on test drives.

God pulls down strongholds.

The power available is dynamics in action.

Do you love me, said three times, is total forgiveness.

Everything that could be over you is already under my God's feet.

God will never send us anywhere where His grace will not meet us.

God overcame space and time. He got us to the other side.

The disciples had 12 baskets of leftovers yet still forget (lest we forget) the miracles.

The safest place is the centre of God's will.

You show me my blueprint.

Don't be a caterpillar, just crawling in and out of church.

Be a pillar, hold each other up.

The word or your will rises up.

Keep the flesh from sliding off the altar.

The butterfly is the inner nature of the cocoon.

The self-righteous approach comes chilled from the fridge.

May my humility not just be too much pride?

Don't die as a seed. Become a forest!

I am stronger on my knees.

Stand in every bit of tight you can get. His yoke is easy.

The storms make the difference to what you find when you reach shore. What will wash ashore?

Same heat that softens the wax, hardens the clay.

Come ye apart – literally came apart as well as step aside the noises and listen to the truth of silence.

What you are building into? What materials are you using?

The world cries out, 'What is the question!'

Morality is replaced by convenience because the foundation is lost.

Hear God, it may be an inconvenient moment but just listen.

Stop looking at the waves.

Wear your very own cloak of memory of prayers said.

Safest place is the centre of your will.

Strengthen the things that remain.

I live through Christ, not circumstances.

God sees to the end of many days, so wait.

Learn the ways of God and find playful joy.

Redirect fear into respect for God.

Erase black thoughts.

To God be the glory.

Jesus come home with me!

I finally stopped long enough for God to catch me.

Take away useless rituals so I can serve the living God.

Mighty strength in clay pot joy.

His hands are the framework on which I hang my day.

At the limit of the possible is sheer delights.

In solitude so quiet, it is deafening. I find Jesus has found me.

He was helpless on the cross, he couldn't move!

My life is not bits of thread anymore, but a picture. It is a framed tapestry not the frayed back full of knots.

Don't water prayer down don't dilute it.

Better shun the bait than struggle in the snare.

Be in the habit of having no habits.

Leap on to the bar of faith.

Get up and run out of the cul-de-sac.

Truth never changes, ever!

Sin fades into the background of my senses. Holy Spirit takes the place of sharp fear.

Ordinary days, extraordinary wisdom.

I realise who I am without you.

God's honour is at stake.

Nestle in Jesus. His wings fits round you perfectly.

Cut it out so no more landing pads of excuses. Transact with God.

I have Jesus to answer at the door.

Do you realise and recognise the power of God!

I will flounder on the sands if I trust my feelings.

God helped me up

The jigsaw is fixed.

He has met us in the Garden.

There is not one broken link on God's chain.

God has brought my mind home!

I get into focus.

I am replanted by the stream of living water!

A diamond is in my hand.

There is a song in all we do, not a deadline.

In tune with Jesus, get rid of the dross.

Be pure glass, nothing can get into it.

A restored poster is pinned up, no uncurling.

I am unstitched and realigned into my truest shape.

I have got back hopeful.

God has reconstructed my portrait.

When you come back into the call you, realise God hasn't changed.

I have caught a vision. Living in ways others haven't begun to learn.

I go through to the other side.
I am entrusted with the secret things of God.
God motivates my living, not my self-interests.
The perfume of Jesus seeps into my clay.
God has pressed into me. I open the presents at the end of my bed.
You have set my feet on a spacious place.
Faith got there first so when grim family of sighs and tears dropped by for a visit, they don't stay long.
Light and truth have led me onto the Holy Hill.
After midnight comes dawn.
God gathers the waters of the sea and puts the deeps into storehouses.
Walk closely with God in the valleys more than the spectacular mountain peaks.
How great is that darkness now your light reigns.
Be convinced and live gently.
A glimpse is mine.
God is holding my mind.
He hears the right cry
Don't blunt my utmost for Gods' highest.
Live the life God intended for you.
Oh Lord, you came back for me.
I stand on the chaos and lift up holy hands.
God has put me back together again.
He bore all the word's sins in one go like us drinking up every last drop of wine.
I stand on the chaos as I'm safe in the cornerstone.
God is my fixed point of reference.
I am exceptional in the ordinary.
Chair is a fixed reference point. I take the devil's wheels off it. He can't push me around anymore.
His plan is a play within a play, I'm out with Him in the deeps.
Tyranny of your individuality goes when you're emancipated about into personality.
God came through for me.
The storms sanctify us, not sink us.

I can buy the field.

It was done in such a way, as never need to be repeated.

I have seen the shape of truth.

Root is gone, cross is in its place.

You have thrown me back to swim again.

Lord, you walk beside me on the shore.

I've crossed the bridge. I'm through the gate of hope and on the edge of glory.

Stop repeating sins.

Live in the grey days despite feelings.

Face Goliath and live!

Great men fall on their strong points, never the weak ones.

Pray as much in good times as well as the bad.

Chiselled bird, now I'm free.

Old self is gone.

Persistent sins will bear the penalties.

Whatever you're willing to walk away from will determine what comes into your life.

Be beautiful and beautifully abandoned to God.

Don't give up all the good things. You're approved and loved.

I rise to the occasion.

Live who you were destined to be.

Despair is the limit of the possible so step out in faith and live.

Receive myself in the fires of sorrow, then I will have leisure to listen and care for others.

Lose the reliance on self and see the Lord.

Narrowest hinges in my hand are more technical than any machinery.

I dance to the right tune.

Fear not for your life only fear that it doesn't begin.

I have touched the hem of his garment.

My worth is that God made me and Christ paid for me.

All is in the Lord, not in the problem.

No more running scared.

An obedience of equal. I am worth it.

Rejection has no hold on me.

The princess is in the palace, how beautiful she is.
Don't mistake the shadows for the reality.
Help me get a grip.
My mind is full of things that deserve praise.
The sky is full of promises.
Love burns away mind sets.
Invisible gas thoughts are gone.
Don't block your imagination.
I don't go off the road.
Loneliness is a disconnection with spiritual self.
Lines have fallen in pleasant places.
I wake up to myself

Summer is the season of perseverance making the roots go deeper and richer.

My cup runneth over – what is in me when I'm bumped? What spills out? Bitterness or joy?

I am a prize possession.

Don't go there – don't even let that thought in!

My broken spirit is healed.

Don't be select listeners. Keep the phone of God's call to your ear.

God called Adam in the cool of the day, not manic, panic heat.

God is my creativity, my peaceful sanctity.

Jesus in Gethsemane needed to pray to get rid of fear.

Prayer means the light is on so don't stumble through the day.

I stay in your frame work.

Make me wise (doesn't mean knowledgeable but to act right at all times).

Be inductive and deductive in Bible reading.

I don't live in the devil's failures. I sing at victories.

Whatever I 'feel', the result will be the same.

Faith is realised hopes that seem unreachable. Keep my faith hot.

I am set free to be holy.

May I distinguish the fundamentals from the trivial?

My mind has limitations you can overcome.

Life stripped to its essentials is freedom.

I drink from the Bible. It gives life to my soul.

I take the filters off, see the truth clearly.

Like a signpost, not to draw attention to itself rather the direction of the city.

Don't let it land in your hair.

The spirit has placed gifts in to my hands – it was cut deep.

I do not need to live in false guilt feelings, guilty when I don't need to.

Devil will try to build up failure in me.

May I punch the top floor button lift of faith and go all the way. Whether I push it trembling or with enthusiasm, the results are the same.

I get rid of excess spiritual and psychological baggage.

In suffering pain wrappings are taken off memories relieved and hearts stirred to allegiances, in largeness of God with them.

Gold refined is my dross resurfaces and 24 carat faith develops underneath.

I throw it all way. It just entangles me.

Loving kindness, not neurotic or commercial.

May I never look through the distorted windows of my prejudice?

You, Lord, never go sour or too shallow to satisfy.

I don't expect from others, Lord, what you alone can give me.

At the limit of the possible is only faith left.

May my desires not colour my thinking.

How can I measure the sway of desires held over the theatre of my mind?!

Holiness allows for my fullest expression of bodily appetites and natural and spiritual gifts.

I let go of my life and let God take control.

The more it is God's fight, the more it is truly mine.

May I serve you God, in what I have to do right now!

Chapter 3
Scenarios

How can we just pour and the glass come? That the "jigsaw" of our lives is not missing any pieces? It is indeed fixed when we still feel just like all the jigsaw pieces jumbled up inside the box. 'Go up to Jerusalem,' the Lord says, and you just feel like a poster peeling off the wall, and then he is the buggy that fixes it back into place. So let's tear up our thoughts as they are just an illusion (as the 80s' song goes). So I pour in faith and expect the glass to come. How Abraham must have felt as he tied Isaac on the altar. I step into the blueprint of my life. I believe my seams of the stitches of the shape I am in are only the total trust in his word alone. I do have a diamond in my hand and I set off again. Oh yes, how many, many times onto this, the sunrise road. I am like that little five-year-old in Cyprus walking through the vines hearing God. Matt 6 says…how much darker is the darkness once you know, you know. Come on after midnight. There is indeed the dawn! Make sure you're ready with your oil lamps full.

God is creation. He is creative so often we do not allow ourselves to live in that place, thinking it is only for the holidays. So we drown in mediocrity and limited our vision in facts and figures of the demanding limiting world. Our work ethos is so dull and monotonous. Only on holidays do we sink our toes into the hot sand and proclaim WOW!!! But each day we have got that. Call this chapter the pop-up picture book. It makes you realise just how close God is every day. Even this second. We stopped reading pop-ups as a child but we can live them. Let us not lose the wonder and awe.

Scene 1: Okay. Feeling just so alone and scared then I look up at the dark sky, all heavy and swollen with clouds just waiting to burst. And then they move and a glint of blue is seen and it is the blue of hope. If I just shift my perception (and my butt), there is hope.

Scene 2: On that smelly tube, yet I can close my eyes and I can live spirit. Then mind. Then Body. That order instead and I am on a shore, walking on that white sand watching the dawn rise with Jesus. And hey, it is my stop.

Scene 3: Checking the door, the oven, the taps and finally realise the finality of the cross Jesus was nailed to the cross, to set me free. I hear the sound of the nails driven into him. The out of control unnecessary of my life is nailed once only to the cross. I let it go. It is over. How much humility. I can feel as he did it once over so my life is a new, free moment. To move freely in away from a mental disorder.

Scene 4: Waiting for the bus I feel a weight in my hand like it is right on the floor, and I look down. There is a diamond in my hand. How am I using my hands to write, to call, to hold, to reach out for you.

Scene 5: Birds in the sky are like angels to me, whenever I see them. I think of how angels are around us all day, protecting us and so I look at the birds and think of how free I am. Their sounds seem so certain too. They fly despite the gravity pull. Can we?

Scene 6: Bones. Yes all discarded every day. I saw a pile of someone's chicken lunch and I just thought of how we waste our lives in negative thoughts and feel like we are worthless and a waste. The bible talks of bones the "dry bones" in the Bible, oh how we need to let the word of God and his truth breath into us…again and again. Our dry bones can live!

Scene 7: Feathers, Yes, seeing a pure white feather every day just floating past my face always dry, always the same length. Even the tube, in the library. Why just one? How did it get there? Such a visible sign such a blessed assurance that I am surrounded by God's love and I am safe, and he is transforming me. He is in my every step, every day.

Scene 8: Roses. Yes, they helped me accept my femininity. We are as beautiful as a rose, just look at the intricacy of a flower. God created us so well. I saw the dots on these mini blossoms, hidden under huge leaves on this tree. And I said to God, why he bothered, as no one will see them but he does his work properly, perfectly. We are wholly put together, and if we abuse that in over indulgence, or we are told we are too vain. God only wants the best. I know I am allowed to be beautiful, as that is God's truth. I pray he sees my beauty in my heart like those dots on those hidden petals.

Scene 9: The way I walk up the road to a corner. That corner is significant as it is a conscious action. I turn it and yes, it is over. I've turned the corners in my life so accept the changes and give God the glory. Have we time to stand and stare? Have we time to use a daily action and apply that to a spiritual discipline? I turn to God.

Scene 10: I take key words out of music and pictures in the media as even these can be used by God and inspire us. And I can see what I mean to God today and divert it to his perspective and his purpose in my life. Especially when you're doing your shopping in the supermarket and there is a song on, what word can you hold onto from that song to remind you of who you are in Christ despite doing the mundane and essential things like shopping?

Scene 11: Looking at adverts: We are allowed things. Yes, we are given the best because God is a great dad and he can only give us the best. So let's use it and praise Him, whatever fabulous things are in our lives. His generosity in revealing Himself to us. So the more you have, live the right humbleness through these fabulous gifts. So dance in joy to his rhythm in the laughter of your child, that designer dress, your gorgeous hunk of a boyfriend, the sound your car makes, the money that keeps on coming.

Scene 12: Walking past a house that is being renovated. To be this new person is quite a lot to take in. So I see it as renovating a house. This analogy helps me cope with all He has done because it is too amazing for words. And I feel dreamlike and God says it is like you are upside down yet really now you are the right way up. And your dream is real so you feel like that, but this is the real relationship, just like falling in love.

Scene 13: So at the cross, the beginning and the end is amazing as he said it is finished. Whenever I used to hear this, I'd be sad, disappointed, fearful as it marked the end to a relationship to people and things in my life, coming to an end. Yet now it is hope as I leave all my out-of-date sell by bags at the cross and it is gone. I don't need to go back and pick them up again. All that rotten mess. Only the good stays as my heart is open to God and His will, it is the crunch time as it is faithful not fear, and that is living the extraordinary in the ordinary and victory happens. We have today's miracles.

Scenario 14: Walking on the sunny side of a street. I am on the Sunrise Road at last, all stumbling blocks are out of path and I face the sunrise and the palms of my hand touch the soul and it is heated. It is the warmth of God himself. I am not going to squander the miracle. I am off the dimmer switch. I am indeed able to be beautiful. Click my heels and be the realest me.

Scenario 15: In an art gallery looking at a huge tapestry. I am the framed tapestry, not the frayed bits of chord and cotton all knotted at the back of the tapestry. God has said I am the front of the tapestry and set in a frame and even the darkest outlines that outline parts of the shapes on the tapestry now define and highlight the shape I truly am. I am indeed drawn up and into the light. I am his art work. I know my redeemer. He frames me. He protects me.

Scenario 16: Standing at a perfume counter. I am perfumed clay, moulded and the scent is sweet. Filtered by God. He has pulled all the grit out, even the tiniest fleck and I am whole and fixed and redefined and shapely and I stand without wobbling and am filled with the water of life and I blossom in air of hope and truth.

Scenario 17: As I punch in my pin number. God was (1) and is (2) and is to come (3). One is unity, two is communion, three is divine, four is seasons, five is completeness, six number of men, seven is perfection, and eight is new beginnings. Oh may we pick up our destiny and walk in truth. What's your number? How many numbers we live by each day: our bus home, at the store, phone, and bank balance. Just get back to these simple numbers. Simple and real.

Scenario 18: As I walk into a room, any room or space, I can say who the leading authority is. The power here and I do not need to give my power away as I come back to Jesus. Give him respect and he has my back and he is the one I answer to.

Scenario 19: Trying on a new coat. I am standing in the God shape. I stay in that place that shape. It is the shape of fresh water as the reservoir drains away, drains all the black thoughts. I am left standing in the promises of Jeremiah 29, a cloak (like an elbah cloak), made up of all friends and family, all memories and people, a promise of God. And I stand on the promise from God to my mum; God said he would save her and her household. Promises that God does say 'I will in no wise, fail you.' There are no doors in this reservoir to open into that debt, weight, fear, the past, OCD. It is a fresh water reservoir, free of those fun-fair crazy house doors. It is the "centre of God's will", the safest place to be. The devil can't reach you if you're in the middle. I am out of the maze of self, into the centre. No more crazy house – wiggly floors (fear), distorted mirrors in the dark (my perception of things) or doors that spring back on me (loneliness). But press on into freshwater and awake. Get out the treasure box for yourself. We tuck it away, we hide it and when someone calls, we get all this love out but we are also allowed to use it. We are allowed as much love as we give away. See God first, experience his overflowing happiness.

Scenario 20: Going back home after 20 years. Awake home vision fellowship. Given to me as I move out of London. Home to write. Back to the house where I first wrote at 17, with the circle tower like a circle of truth, a ring of my mother's wise words. I am full circle home. Awake, how you have been asleep in debt, weight, fears, past and OCD. Just so asleep in despair and drink. Vision – yes you do not need to squander the miracle anymore, nor be on the dimmer switch. Be in the light. Yes come out of the darkness. Put the hinges back on reconnect to the wonder and stay in fellowship. Found a drama group home with my parents, going back to my brethren church. God has finally got me there. Hedged in a life on the Sunrise Road.

Scenario 21: I am home. I am not deceived by any angels of desire, and ego. Indeed the low self-esteem has gone and God's love, Hesed, his blood, sweat in Gethsemane has washed me clean. I do not have any spirits of fear in me but rather spirit of love, power, self-discipline and sound mind. I do indeed erase black thoughts. I am then healed. The devil is a roaring lion but is defeated. I do not need to be deceived by unbelief.

Scenario 22: I am pulled up. I am so exposed in the bright light. I am held upside down. All my wriggly roots. Yet God is holding me upside down and right mind up. All wriggly raw roots exposed. Yes I am exposed in order to be replanted. Will I realise the land to root and settle myself in. So I am replanted in God. I am pulled up, held in mid-air. High as eagles wings in air, in bright truth. I am soaked in Christ. Soaked so I am not going to snap. I am not brittle. I am not so withered that the world could influence me. Oh Lord, I pull myself together. Oh put all the right bits back together.

Scenario 23: Sitting at the kitchen table looking out the window. My chair has no wheels. I am fixed. I do not need to veer out on my own. If I stay in the centre of gods will then I am in his perfect peace. A fixed reference point. I don't kick against the goads. If I kick I only hurt myself, what is the point? Let them prod me to keep me on the narrow way. Get me realigned and when I get up and go into the world, I go in God's stride. His steps are restful and peaceful, not a manic chaos.

Scenario 24: Going through a maze hedge at a castle. I'm like a maze, even to myself. You always show me a way out my mental despair, and lack of faith in myself. It is over. I pick up right humbleness, not low self-esteem. The humbleness that says "with God I can". May I be faithful in the little things you gave me to do, like calling someone each day or learning to save money. I do have my hands on the plough. Yes, this is my field of faith. I plough what is here in front of me and look ahead. I do not need to think no more on it (whatever those "its" are). Like gravel in your shoes, they are gone. I can stand up inside. I can climb out of my tree. This equation is truth itself. Know it to be the true and use its formula to create truth. I want to be spent for you (worn out to my last 1p, only for you).

Scenario 25: As the areophane takes off. Come up higher. Am I in a habit of developing your disposition and conduct in my personal character in my life? I live up to the highest I know I can do. I still climb higher. Not climbing as the world demands, where nothing is ever going to satisfy, the always looking for something more. In the end not daring to move as the debt has mounted and you're clinging to a pinnacle. Live for the Lord obey his ways and he takes you to a large place not spinning on a pinnacle. It is about climbing the "more than" life with Jesus. So arriving on a huge great landing where it is easy to move. See how last year at this time, compared to this time. See how much higher you have indeed come. My insight of my character, the emancipation of my personality has indeed come up so much higher. It is so wonderful to feel and know we are hid with Christ in God. Yes, my mind is hidden and the devil can't find it. Climbing in my stance, attitude, perception and disposition, disconnected and connected on the hotline to Jesus. My lifeline is the lord, I can climb up higher.

Scenario 26: Coming out the cinema after an afternoon film. I came out into the light that is grace itself. It is a light that is always on, an almost too beautiful, all so beautiful light. The light is revealed at its shiniest when in the darkest nights. Everyone's darkest nights are different but we can see the brightness of the stars despite. They are switched on for us as we believe in God. So we get an "on" button. Never forget the level we can rest on is higher than the demons that haunt us. So don't live in needless pain. You're up higher so why do or stay in a mindset or why do or be in a place. You have a home, a cleft of rock so why live on the streets. Start realising the resources available to you. You wait to win the lottery when really, you already won. Start using, living in, accepting just what the best is. God gives us the best over the good. We still have some of our old smells, our old clothes but we don't need to be deceived anymore. Start throwing away, kicking it off your heels, the old things. Faith in God will connect the truth in your heart with your feet. So get up and go. You have a destination, a purpose and a place of rest.

Scenario 27: First day of spring. I live our seasons of my life. In spring, I live in hope and promises. I pull up all the weeds and trim and realign and rearrange my mental furniture. In summer I go for it. I get spiritual grit against the world. I listen to the way god talks to the insight of my character. In autumn, I bear fruit and prepare myself so I can be fruitful. And in winter, I have a season of rest. I prune myself and stay close to my creator who keeps me nourished and ever hopeful.

Scenario 28: Hearing my own heartbeat after a run. My heart is restless till it finds its rest in you. Hope deferred maketh the heart sick. My mind needs to accept what my instincts knew all along. The rest is dung. Can I realise that now at last? So by believing it, is that I pour and then the glass comes. This is the intimacy of going and doing. I choose to live in domestic courtesy. I can choose the most excellent way, closest to Jesus alone. Intimate with him. People are shadows so say no. be like Caleb an overcomer, he saw just grasshoppers. Accept the charity of fellowship. Awake. You have a vision, stay in fellowship a delightful friendship with the Holy Spirit. This is the spine of my life as the cross spelt out these words and wiped me free from stains. I use the same beautiful energy to rejoice and praise my god, as I would to get ready to go to an event or meet the Queen. How honouring am I in my every day preparations, to meet and live for God. Will I do for God in ambition and energy what I did for my old life? In consistency, I find a covenant, an agreement sealed with God. With God, I always find the harbour and come in from the storms.

Scenario 29: trying to learn to knit. Oh the image of being framed, not the frayed back of the tapestry, not the wiggly upside down uprooted soil. I am a new me in that you have unstitched me and unpicked and realigned my image with yours and so despite the emotions, it seems like chaos is truly over. You told the moon where to stand in the sky. You made the tide just come up to the line of the shore the right amount of push and pull. In any sorrow I either find myself or destroy myself. So with both hands I hold onto the self you made me to be in this moment, even in sorrow I can glorify your name. I unlearn and see the rest as shadows they have no power over me. Oh all of you Lord, none of me. The stance attitude perception of it. Why should there be a gap at all! Deliverance comes in trouble, in sorrow. I have life as I overcame the strains, is the strength in the strain is life, liberty and joy. I overcame fear to take that step. No more spending in the world that is exhaustion, rather spending spiritually is strength in this strain of the minute. I come from a God point of view, not a common sense one. Nothing is impossible with God. I jump, skip and hop.

Scenario 30: When your best friend leaves. Your Elijah will go and you can go on without Elijah. Alone at your Jordon, no one else there. A total separation. Just you and God. Oh to be mature in the Lord with Jesus' survival skills. God has not forgotten me. I come off my throne, self-off the throne and take up the cross meant for me. I don't let anyone take my crown. My blessings are mine. I can be alone at Jericho. I take the initiative and trust God that even with just you, you can do great things. Alone at my Bethel I am at my wits end and at the beginning of God's wisdom. I will not panic but stand true to God. I use my Elijah cloak and God will bring the truth out. I will not look for Elijah no more. I am at one with God, slotted in. I do not need to be in elementary panic prayer. I may get to breaking point but it does not break my confidence in Him.

Scenario 31: Sorting out the clothes in my wardrobe. What is hanging up in your wardrobe? There are rich clothes of temperament, personal affinity, relationships of heart and mind and you sometimes add accessories of expressions of sorrow. You need to clear your wardrobe out and undress yourself morally before God so all possessions and the "just you human" all belongs to God. Take my will, Lord. May the essentials in my wardrobe include having a disposition like yours? Oh criticise my dress sense. Yes I am not too sensitive to hear your comments. Take my self-love and dress me in devotion to you. May you shine through as my label, my designer? My style comes from you as I walk down the catwalk of life.

Scenario 32: Repainting and decorating a room. It's like renovating "that" room, the one you left till last. You have to do this yourself, (determinedly demolish), the sin like the layers of 1940s' wallpaper you have to strip it away. It might take a layer of skin with it like a super wax in a beauty parlour. They say no pain, no gain. You are on a mission to neglect, to starve, to ignore certain elements of your human nature and some you fight with the violence only found in the Holy Spirit strength. Truth oh yes, it's slightly messy and then in other areas, just stand still. No one to compromise with, no to striving. To sort it out. Just stand still and see. It's like you have taken that step up and, in your disposition, like renovating a room. Only through moral choices "don't go there" will you find your holy character. Do you have an account with Jesus, then get this "room" of yourself sorted, every nook and cranny realigned. Oh yes, live by discipline not by impulses. Instead of bouncing off impulsive ideas, stay in the heartbeat of God like Moses said, let's number our days and gain a heart of wisdom. Do you realise the responsibility of transformation. Can you finish the renovating in that last area of your life?

Scenario 33: Planting up the garden. Okay, certain words can be like a packet of seeds, for example each letter of that word is an individual seed, all mixed up and will totally blossom. In my brunch is firstly "awake" that conjures up, that finally I have surfaced up out of the sea. I can breathe again. Another blossom bunch of seeds: jigsaw. All the pieces found. A promise to my mum all those years ago that her and her household will be saved. I am off the dimmer switch: "Home" places like Holland Park, Gospel Hall in Tunbridge Wells in the 1980s. My faith planted there as a young child. Oh and returning to it 30 years later to see how truth rang out from its walls. Oh what a wasted time leaving such a blessed fellowship for the city bright lights. Now I am attached to the vine of my home, living with parents attached in noble beauty at last. I have come home. I seek first. And I don't need needless pain that of fighting against the goads. I got to see Ian and Christa who saved our family in Cyprus before they died. Meeting myself coming back at a play in London and seeing a diamond in my hand in the tube. My hand fell with the weight in it. To see my mind like a damaged fishing net all fixed. To have the tapestry, all the threads of consequences now add up framed, not frayed. To be perfumed clay moulded into realest shape I shall ever be. "Fellowship" means I am back where I first begin in the place God meant for me. Thank God there is still time to rectify and resolve and reconnect like a whole re-wiring of a house like the planting of all these seeds, now I can truly see what I looked for so far away from this place. These truths, now all I ever wanted is blossoming and I am in a moral frontier. The blossoms grow and change the landscape. I am now of use for God. I am mended nets, my inner souls self is in balance with my personality. I am Him healed, the kink is out of my mind, the arrows or victory land straight and I know I am free of fear for God sweated even blood for me in the Garden of Gethsemane. I bank my faith in the character of God and pour and the glass comes. May I stay now free of ever repenting of my repentance, even in the midnight hour, the 4.00am despair? I can call on the name of the Lord. At last, I am constructed. So hid with God the devil can't find me. I now have come up higher and do not try to steady myself on a pinnacle but there is a plateau with ample room to live and grow.

Scenario 34: A reflecting moment as I can't sleep. Okay, what does my inner man look like? What about a Bethlehem? Can I be like the nativity scene we see in churches or we put up over Christmas? To be surrounded by genuine peace and heat of warmth of love and concern and simplicity. No airs or graces. Just like that scene. Christ formed in me. Do I truly live in a new birth, a rising up out of the old self? Christ comes into this world. He wasn't evolved out of history. He came in from outside and so he comes into me from outside and takes his place with the God shape, part of me. With the star above me in my inner Bethlehem, the light, the centre of the light becomes closest and I can see the truth and how much darker is the darkness of sin and how it so deceives with its illusion of heightened emotions that I think are happiness. It is in my inner Bethlehem that the severest battles can be won. I will never win them at 4.00am with a bottle or two of wine inside me, but instead to meet my blessed saviour and be held. I never need to lose my peace or run into the world so broken and trapped by low self-esteem. My decision with God is a serious contract. It is my obedience to the heavenly vision that makes me a slave of Christ and not a slave of the world's point of views. The scene is set, the curtains are drawn back, the life begins and the unveiling of real truth. The dust covers reveal the beautiful furniture and the home is warm and lived in. I am never the same again, all is a new sound. Have you heard, felt, seen and lived in your own Bethlehem. I do.

Scenario 35: Watering my plants. Add it and it grows, whether it be a bank balance or feeding a new born baby. Now we're "Christians", what does that mean? How can we add, how can we grow, can we ever become like a granite stone, so firm, so solid in our faith with our heart kept like a child's in innocence, truth and love? What are we adding daily to help us grow? The growth draws and calls and holds up into place the realest self. Like stripping the husk off a corn or a sweet corn, the old mud caked, dried up life flicks away and the true God shaped realest life emerges. Can we flick the mud away, rinse it off till it dissolves and we can't pick it up again in a wistful nostalgia or insecure moment of doubt. How close will we let the chisel get to scrape out the driest, awkward corners of ourselves? Do you not realise your blockages causes the delay of blessings. Do we realise we have been purified, the grit has been taken out of our makeup and we are as smooth and strong as granite. This is the strength of our faith walk. By adding God, we can grow up into our God shape and take bold steps of faith.

Scenario 36: Breakfast. You get these cereals packed with a mixture of three or four or five ingredients of goodness. A multigrain bar or smoothie. So with our faith walk, lots and lots of our God walk is done in a mixture of goodness and truth. Trying to be holy, we are written in the book of life, we are marked in him with a seal. The potential promise and purpose are all clear. We unlearn like starting a new healthy eating plan and it is difficult at first as food tastes funny without salt or mayonnaise. But despite relearning or learning for the first time how to eat a balanced diet, is like the undoing and remaking me that Jesus does because he puts me back on the potter's wheel and I come out in a completely new shape, reformed and an instrument for noble purposes. Our new shape can be seen from all angles like in those 360-degree mirrors. All is in the light, nothing is in shadow and we can let God measure us up in his grace, not in judgment. It is hard to give up certain things that taste nice or seem OK. But then we can stand up the scales, see the difference in our shape, our weight and recognise that the letting go broke the dam of our comfort zone and got us up into life. We can refit the truths we stopped daring to dream, get back to the size we were always meant to be.

Scenario 37: Letting down a Lillo. Letting the air out like a pressure cooker top. Or a steam/fried filled room full of smoke. By letting the air, steam and smoke out, the sight becomes clearer, the place in ourselves gets back to normal. We let the world fill us up with air, empty promises usually financial or from untruthful people who don't even realise as they are so used to living a lie. Their lies have become their truths. When life's chaos have taken us so high in the sky of false hopes, letting out the air, coming back to land safely in deep peace and joy is an effort, a mental effort to keep on keeping on letting the air out.

Scenario 38: Holding a cup of tea. We all have a cup full. Life gives us so many things, some we don't expect or some that are quite lovely surprises. It's when someone jolts it that reveals our inner hearts state of affairs. What spills up and over the top, does it land like acid and burn? We speak out bitterness and hate from our hearts. Or can it spill and like nourishing water flower itself into something utterly inspirational in someone else's life? If I'm jolted, will I speak an unkind word? Am I just full of myself, a stagnant out of date sauce that's truly good for nothing and gives everyone else a stomach ache? Oh to be consistent in seasons as well as out of season. Get jolted today, test out your faith. What is your heart full to the brim with?

Scenario 39: Mathematics. Can God be our equation? Can you be a difficult sum that even you don't quite know how it all got into that place in your space and now it's a huge sum, full of complex analysis to unfold it and reach an answer? He can do that, He can highlight and take each part, deal with each section and deal with each part of the equation. Nothing is too difficult. Subtle loving help like someone explaining a math's question he can find a way to order and solve the complexity of the sum. He knows the right way of living. He orders our steps, putting into place each part of who we are. Like an equation must have the right answer so must God as he is truth. This is how God realigns us so that we know, through obedience, the compulsion to love. The love Jesus has for us makes him work for our good, bringing our whole self into the right answer, the only answer that is right. Let him minus and divide you and bring just the very best of you together into the answer you have been looking for all your life.

Scenario 40: Choosing a perfume. Sanctified means I'm cut and implanted with order, sanity, holiness. How do I release my fragrance? It is by being broken. From huge brokenness the deepest fragrance can come. Will you let him break you? All the strongholds in your life? His pierced hands will do the breaking and it will be gentle. The fragrance will influence all those that come your way, even before you say anything about Jesus, they will know you are different. You have been broken and released, no more confined in a restricted area. No more swilling about in your own selfish desires. When self is smashed, the best part of you is released, you benefit, as you are free and not clinging too tightly anymore to world values. God got us up and out of slavery to this world. Now be an empty clean vessel that he can fill with blessings and favour. Remember as a Christian, you now have treasures in earthen vessels, in clay jars and its Jesus' fragrance pouring through us.

Scenario 41: Noise outside in the middle of the night. The midnight hour that 12pm, or 4am or 5am slot when the darkness consumes you, it ebbs and flows around you and mingles with the darkest fears and thoughts that break open like an egg and run out of your mind. Once broken, unable to relock or gather up again, they spill out into the midnight hour darkness, lost in layers of more darkness. The internal individual life that is the most vulnerable at this midnight hour. It is a time of solitude and loneliness and we hope to hear a knock, a knock of love of hope of justice. All of us need an answer of sorts to allow us to awaken to the dawn, to live fully and alive and fulfilled. Have you heard your knock? Reach the door of your haunted midnight house. Hear the knock and answer to Jesus. He has the answer. He carries the light with him.

Scenario 42: Having a garden party. So much in our gardens can inspire us as to the beauty and love of God and how he has good things for us. How we can step onto soft sun warmed grass with our bare feet and off the harsh gravel ground of the world's superficiality. God's carpet of grass, with all its activities and daisies makes us certainly reconnect to the wonder of this world. It is staying in this space that we can hear Him in all the softness of the gardens sounds. Our mind, like a big knot of wool, can untangle and rewind itself into order at last. As our feet soak in the grass freshness, we can reclaim our tune and step in time again to the pace of life. To feel well watered and delicate like a well-watered garden. To know who you're attached to, the connection to the vine, the truth of God. To know you're not meant to give your branches away. Just the fruit you bear. To stand up in all areas of your life, like a flower, tall and strong in the garden, swayed by wind but never breaking its stem. Doubts and emotions may try to dominate but the truth remains the same.

Those weeds need to be pulled up immediately. Look at the intricate beauty and detail found in the garden to see how splendid the beauty of God is, if we would only claim it. Our colours await. Also don't let wild strawberries or weeds overrun your garden. Be careful what may try to come in and consume. Live out the immense joy of your faith in life like a blossoming garden. Do you have parties in your soul? Let God just water you fully, soak you. You don't need to be anything. Just let it be. Let your seeds of hope, all you have dreamed of, take root and then see how they flower, growing up and changing the whole landscape. Remember, He hedges us in safety. Like the most delicate flower in the garden, it is safe and secure. Enjoy your time with God, like the sitting in the dusk of the day and watching the sun go down and the stars come out. Remember your roots reach the source, wherever you have landed. You can cope as your source is God's living spring. Like all his flowers, God has not and cannot make a mistake. Look at the detail in each variety. Whatever season you find yourself in, trust God. Be happy with the flower or plant He has made you to be. Don't compare yourself to another variety. Let God prune you. Don't try to do the job yourself. It's so good to allow yourself to be part of the messiness of life. Like a garden, it all can't be perfect yet to know you belong is everything? You can live with a sense of care freeness as God is in control and He is most careful with you. Let off your sweetest fragrance. So have a vision of you in your garden and recognise the possibilities and bloom. The world needs love and beauty!

Scenario 43: Finding a lost piece of jewellery. God hides treasures. There are hidden treasures all over the world. He is a God of fun and excitement, like a hide and seek game. Everything we ever needed is somewhere on this planet if we would just open our eyes to see.

Scenario 44: Standing on a bridge. I am finally on my designated platform and I can enjoy the view, the climb is over. I am fit enough to zoom down the highway now, free from roadblocks and join the parade for I listened to the voice and heard the sound of Jesus saying, 'Come up higher.'

Scenario 45: How I feel inside. I can live in a palace within. I can leave the mindset of fears and the past. I am my shape now, no one can sway me from God's voice (Genesis 17 v1). Walk before me and be though perfect. My lifestyle is sanctified. I can turn my face completely the other side and look into the horizon of my vision. In the rhythm of his favour, not the chaos of my fears.

Scenario 46: Waiting for a train. It's about laying the tracks like laying railway tracks. Once you lay them, His power then can come. Are you laying your tracks?

Scenario 47: As seconds tick by. Yes, heaven came through to Earth and God will raise you up in due time. Go to the ocean with more than a teaspoon. Break the alabaster perfume box. Get pressed into your blueprint. Don't get vomited out of the disbelief Jonah whale. Stand up and walk through your Red Sea and stand up inside in the land of promise. You don't need to be numb anymore. I reach out like Jabez did into another kind of life.

Scenario 48: Polishing my shoes. God has put the shine in it. He's polished and sealed his promises. Be like Caleb who did not see giants but saw grasshoppers. 'I am well able to overcome'. Cast away the doubts that limit God's goodness. Rather do a grand display of Christ's gentleness today. Since in this ordinary day. Don't let others set boundary lines. The strain of waiting for God is over. Jesus has met me at the end of myself and given me my shine back.

Scenario 49: Reaching for the light switch. You're up on a level, you can't get pulled down. No one can get a hold of you. Climb up there. Have a vision and climb into it. I am home in usefulness and safely on my small piece of the planet designated for me. Wherever you feel anxious, go for the switch. Just turn the light of truth on if it ever gets dark. It is the only light in which you will see your way clearly. Remember, don't draw things up from the dregs of your well. Draw things down from heaven. Never go deeper to find peace. Always look up.

Scenario 50: Going for a walk. It's great to walk on warm soil, knowing it is put there by God alone. He has sifted my soul and replanted me and I don't trip up over anything anymore, as he has taken all the boulders out of my way. It is a whole new ground in God's favour. The giants are too big to miss. Only God flings me now, not chaos. So I'm no empty pod. He can fling me wherever. I have stood up and stand up, walking on both legs. I have been helped up the holy hill.

Scenario 51: Walking away from sin. God is the answer. If you try to make your mark, you will attract erasers. Stay in wisdom perfecting holiness in the fear of God. We are brought into living communion with God and that is life. I stand on the heads of lust and fear. I came apart to be whole in God.

Scenario 52: Seeing everything through the cross perspective. On the cross, as the nails went in, they carved my name on the wood with the same faith. I cry to my Lord and my God as he cried on the cross. Push all your emotions to their logical conclusions and if the outcome is sin, spit it out. I don't work out a greater vision on a lower level. Let it have the right place in your life. So as not to end up a sentimentalist. Be in your hour of insight. God will adjust everything. Be amazed by what he does. Keep inside your miracle despite the grey of the day. Let butterflies flutter off. Stay in your blooming vision with purified hope as the water running over everything, refreshing it. Come up higher, a great table. Land awaits, he elevates us into a greater space when the devil elevates us, and we totter on a pinnacle not daring to move. You can move indeed dance in praise and awe for Jesus endures, not moving on the cross, to give you freedom and life worth living.

Scenario 53: Cleaning the ash from the fire place. Don't need to scatter your faith. Have spiritual grit. No more divided heart to hallow victories. God alone knows how to pick up all the pieces. So crash into the heartbeat of God. I can go back to zero. For out of the ashes, He can create a future for me. He carries my burdens, he shoulders them, he helps me carry it one shoulder each his and mine. He leapt over it all. I am not consumed. His compassion never fails. The pins are gone, nothing pins me down. I can stay safe now in God's shaped words of life

Scenario 54: Arriving at your destination. Like Numbers 27, Zelophehads daughters got their inheritance. My hurricane has turned into God's breath. It is a turning point and life will never be the same again. I am now disinterested in that particular emotion. It is pulled away from me. I can slide down my rainbow and dance step by step on stars. So to love in the inspiration of your vision, the Jericho walls have finally come down and I am here all along. My sad, sweet self is gone and in its place is discernment. I go beyond the grasp into the 'more than' of faith. Like Jacob, I am finally broken in my old strength. I run at my giants. I can see the uncircumcised sins on which I do not shipwreck myself any more. I do not cast off restraint. I ask for moral incentive. I awake in the freshness of my vision. I move out and on with God into my inheritance.

Scenario 55: How big is your idea of God? Interrupt your day with praise. Abandon negative thoughts. Put them in the bin outside your mind. Trade in your good or God's best. At the limit of the possible, Lord, you raise me up. Birth a full term vision. Focus on finishing (Judges 8 v4). Get to your Jordan and cross it. Keep God on speed dial and leap into the venture. Be haunted by God alone (Exodus 14 v21). God is up all night driving the sea back. Each of us can walk on dry land.

Scenario 56: Phone call home. Take a deep, spiritual breath and get the dread out. Work out what God had worked in, it's as natural as breathing! God had put the crown of life on your head. He protects the simple hearted and I am out in the deep on the swelling tide of God's purpose. When God puts you out there, you are safe. Don't go there of your own accord. You can sit down now in your heavenly vision. Strive and strife is over your real life, your real life has started. You are caught in the net of God. Don't swerve to the left or right. Let the world now stand aside to let you pass, as at last, I know where I'm going. Dust yourself off and be altogether his (Genesis 31 v13). He orders me back home.

Scenario 57: The Verdict. Learn to hear the sound of the voice of God. He will do what He has promised. Stand up in the docks, loyal to your friend, Jesus. His honour is at stake. I was derailed but He has put me on the tracks. Now God's mouth is at my ear. I look at what lies in me apart from the grace of God. Let the Ananias's recognise the changes in your soul to recognise the miracle in your heart. A miracle encounter is not a waste of time. I hang onto it by the skin of my teeth. I build now with gold bones, connected to calm. I am apprehended (Philippians 3 v12). I am held in his grip for such a time as this. May my heart, nerves, personality blaze and glow with devotion. Burn my lips. Take all my concentrated sins, clean and polished and restored. Judge and Jury declares to the Lord I am so valuable.

Scenario 58: Waiting is over. Joy is my background music. You, Lord, have held onto my original destiny like a lost property department for me to claim it. You, Lord, have helped me up. Like a rod has a bud (Number 17 v5). I am upright and upmost for His highest. Do we make that effort to be noble? Stay in that God shape – don't get side-tracked. Finally, I met you, Lord, like a bus I've been waiting for ages. For I can stand among the ruins of my life and know your company is right beside me. I am rehabilitated. Nothing can penetrate my identity, like I found myself at last. The holy spirit sieves, yes purifies within all my unploughed land is broken up, the deepest roots uncover the thriving bulbs that need to be in the darkest soil so there is where they burst, pierce through and bloom. You take the overgrown worry weeds and give me a backdrop of joy. My heart is in the right season. I reclaim all of my lost property.

Scenario 59: Across the border. I fit now like a new dress size. I fit into a whole new pattern and I fit through the gateway at the moral frontier like a checkpoint. I am stamped and am free to cross the frontier (Mark 6 v45 v52). At last, I have crossed to the other side. I am a barrier breaker because I do believe like the lady in (Matt 15 v27) and Rahab in Joshua 2 v14. The Lord will tear the sky apart and come down. Michelangelo painted the ceiling, not the floor. No one can break the strides of God. The clouds I see are just the dust of his feet. My scaffolding has gone and I enter the big, compelling and the "more" of God.

Scenario 60: No more screaming. The Holy Spirit can get that deep in me and realign purity. I can let go of hysterical spirituality and give up emotional addictions. I am no longer a three-year-old feeling of lost in the supermarket. I am a polished arrow, concealed in his quiver, safe yet ready to hit the mark and display his splendor like David. I use what I know best, my sling and five stones. I live a vital, simple life. My limp comes only from the slightest touch of God. A brokenness from God makes us whole.

Scenario 61: Refiners fire. God stabs at the thing that must go. God has built me into the cornerstone. Make sure there is no leakage that the net doesn't break, for such a time as this. Get the bloom of the touch of the Lord. May you be an unaffected loveliness and be inscribed with "Dedicated to the Lord" so stop looking at the waves. My disposition is nourished by Christ alone. Pull up the thorns. Don't sink back to anything lower. Find the key to the smallest attic door and reconnect to your song. God finds our keys that unlock freedom. Squeezed by Jesus alone, so nothing has to terrify us. The old yeast has been thrown out. The spiritual blacksmith has got me back into shape.

Scenario 62: Making a decision. Can we live Ark shut led decisions and measure up to the standard when God calls us, when the strain comes, can I be relied upon by God. Can I grow the size of my faith to match the destiny for me? Can we live the inner beauty and smell the wonder of love and praise, feeling so weak and small. Do we plug into the God socket? Get up out of the Desert of Param. You don't need any more rest and don't return back to the running steadily in the haphazard surroundings of what I used to be. The Lord's arm is not shortened that he cannot save. Make your life simply the vision of perceiving God's will. Plant the seed in your promised land (John 12 v32). What God asks us to do is always greater than the resources we start with. God insulates us in the middle of temptations to prevent transmission and detaches me, he finds us and puts us on his shoulder so carrying us home. I have a 212 attitude as at 212, water boils and steam is produced which creates power such as for a locomotive, so I retain the possessions of my personality.

Scenario 63: Being heard. God has leant down from heaven to hear you. He airlifts us out of floods. He springs clean us. Don't needlessly torment yourself. He gives us trials, not temptations. Can you we get through these tests? The tests turn my bones to gold. The false partition walls are down, the fear is just an emotion. You don't have to let the devil breath surprise you. Don't let negative emotions run amok in your life. The Holy Spirit has the controls. He can out-pour rest and bequeath peace but don't look for the right thing in the wrong place. You wouldn't go into the kitchen to take a shower!

Scenario 64: Fighting. My wings might be way too small but God's breath blows me high up into freedom. He dismantles the cage. No angel is ashamed to speak his name. He shakes that thing off my heel. So press on like getting into a lift or on a plane and don't look back. Name and shame the trash. Give up your ashes for beauty. Take the unknown step. Stop pouring into leaking cisterns. Oh are you amazed and feel quite odd at what God has done? Don't be an uncontrolled, bridle, Oh Lord, do not take your hand off me. What you can walk away from will determine what God can bring to you. Do you dance the depth, width and length of his favour? Do you know what is worth fighting for? Walking with the Lord alters the atmosphere and handcuffs the sin that so easily sways us, so evict sin out and reach out, stretch up into the blessed life.

Scenario 65: Eviction notice. God has evicted sin from my life. It is an order to be obeyed for He has the last word on the matter. I can now be the more that I was made for. He strides in and alters the atmosphere. Like Enoch did do we walk with God? What I now walk away from will determine what God will indeed bring to me. Leave the evicted place. It is a mere pigsty. A palace awaits you. You may feel odd and amazed by what God has done. The truth cannot be altered. It is deliberate. Persistent and expectant! God knows what it is you need to pick up and to let go and don't look back. You're out of there, it has no hold on you anymore. God alone has his hands all over you now. You walk in newness of light. Yes, into a whole new life. Switched on, plugged in, everything lights up. Nothing now is in the shadows. You let go of the spirit of fear as God has given you a spirit of adoption and your home in him. Like the prodigal son, your home and it isn't "give me". It is now "make me." Oh He can make you the realest you. I am taken by surprise today, flung out and it is good. I will not sink back to something lower ever again. Never need to go back to that place ever again.

 Scenario 66: Free. It's been axed at the root. You can get that thing off your heel. The cage has been dismantled. You can blaze a trail. God has taken out your trash. You now know it's not what you can believe, it is what you can obey. Oh Lord, please do not take your hands off me. What you walk away from will determine what God can bring you. You still have what God put in you, like a bank balance. Nothing has been taken out even though through life, you lost so much. You are still the same value. As I get into God's stride, he alters the atmosphere. I rejoice under the constant pressure as when it tests the reality, the truth is revealed. At the cross, is only possibilities? You can put your feet back on higher ground. When you see his scars and you see scars that are matching. Oh in the cave you are freed from all your fears. Be soaked and rooted so when the strain comes, you won't snap but spring up.

 Scenario 67: Learning a language. Sin speaks a dead language. The Lord knows those that are on his. Satan can't steal anymore what God says is mine, despite the hunted feeling. You are not controlled by the opinion of others. I do not turn from God and be swallowed by what was meant for my growth. I am prepared for God's adjustments. He spelt them out on the cross. Let down your net on the other side and see what you catch hold of. Be at the starting line, in the quiet mood of God's rules. I don't have any more leakage. I step up into my vision. I am apple safe as the apple of his eye. No one, nothing can touch me. Sin is now unemployed, I am now employed by Jesus. The Lord owns my mind, my hands. He is the new tenant. I'm in it yet lifted up beyond and taken to the above. As God is in the ascendant, compulsions go.

Scenario 68: In the workshop. I am at the end of myself. Never to be moved again. Now there is gold and perfume where there used to be darkness and stench. The Holy Spirit fills in the gaps, he coats and flavours and fills in the gaps. I can score a victory goal. I can recognise him on the shore. No more wandering, no more throwing my body at imaginations and affections. All has been vanity. Lord has made all the wrongs right. He has given me the most. Like liquid gold and silver, I am back into shape. He takes the hooks of self-despairs like hooks in your lower lip, He takes them out. He shakes us free from limits and He hides us where the devil can't find us. The natural man sheds his skin in the desert and leaves the end of himself there.

Scenario 69: Untangled nets. Only in the desert is there enough expanse to see the complete vision and the sunrise and the enormity of it. You have to go to the desert where the tyranny of individuality leaves you and you are emancipated into personality. God breaks your mental nets only to fix you. Any boulders in your way, you can pick up and throw them to the side till all that lies scattered finally are those pieces that are your truest identity. You are whole again and realise all the realest you was under a huge pile of debris and you had forgotten, it was so long ago. May we stand the test of time slicing away all that is not meant to be? Lord, your words they are actual life. Use the sword of peace, not a sort of peace no more. God sits down with me and fixes the holes in my life. He actually sits down to fix and finish the job of "me"! My soul is in tune and he hears the merest cry, finally light flickers through the shutters and everything else is in shadows. My miracle is the mended nets of my mind and personality. From frayed to a framed masterpiece. Fixed nets.

Scenario 70: Blowing up a balloon. From the distress of pressure to enlargement and into liberation, embracing the horizon of abundance. A life that I own is mine now. You are the main shape that all my life fits onto, like a main key piece of the jigsaw, central is you Lord, and I can remake it with you at the centre. I am out of the tide, I do not need to get my feet wet anymore. Discipline has broken my will and released and coloured my spirit. There is now colour in my soul. My life no more lives a lie. Today is the beginning of everything. As I pull up my nets, they are filled with sweet surprises. Oh to live in the divine mornings of meeting with the Lord, before the worldly settings build up like stage sets around you. Don't be snared by them, you don't need to entertain the world on false sets anymore. I am rehabilitated. Look now at what you have left behind. Your feet are facing favour and He has filled up your horizon. You are out of the cell of your own limits. The hidden root of unbelief and fear is dragged into the light.

Scenario 71: Getting the post. Bind all attachments that are not of God to the horns of the alter. Then your undisturbed heart is protected today. Do the tasks nearest so we get hold of God, not necessarily the answer, the intense concentration on God. At last, your roots have hit the river and your will is broken, not your spirit. Let us deliberately turn our imagination to God. It is a WOW won-now life turned around. It is the laying of the tracks. Lay the right tracks on which the power can come. Realise the power that can run on those tracks. Let loose your vision, the right things are bound in heaven so God can loose the right things on Earth. Post to Heaven, do you bind up and post the right things to Him? He can release the blessings from heaven. You then get to break the alabaster box. The truth, whole and broken will pour out.

Scenario 72: my River through the desert. Stand in the middle of the Red Sea. It might be a debt of fear and horror of sorts when the world feels like the Red Sea all around you. Remember you are Ark-shut in, so walk out into the thing. Just get up, just do the next thing. You rise higher as you arise and obey. Remember how safe you are like a bookmark in God's hands folded into his pages as he reads you. You're riding into your destiny so safe and hidden. You can take off the training wheels, now no roadblocks and just ride. You have found the honey, past the pain of the bee stings. Jesus is a suddenly God. He is passing by and you can expect a miracle today. The grand displays of self is over because of grace. I am now a right instrument with the right words to my tune. From strain, I've been sieved and strained into wholeness, no bits, no grit. The Holy Spirit is my guide on this truth road where I can be wild and extravagant for Jesus, only like the eagle I break the calluses off my beak on the rock of Christ and pluck 70,000 feathers today. I am renewed today. I stay in the switched-on position. Today, the Lord draws you at out like a stain on a dress. He has finally walked this way and called me by name. You have given me treasures in darkness, riches stored in secret places. I am jumping and leaping. It is at the point of hurt, is the revelation. Despite a tender, frail plant, I know my roots have hit the source. I have learnt in the dark so can now speak out in the light. It is all about the depths of my roots, not the height of my branches. The point of hurt hits the centre and begins the beginning of everything. No more stumbling on a cluttered road as it is now cleared, so now live worthy of the calling you have received. Look back and see you're through the Red Sea on dry land and your roots have hit the source.

Chapter 4
Alphabet

A-Z

A single repeated AAA or PPP......when I am rushing in the morning and the whole effort of reading my Bible, meditating on a passage from scripture is too daunting. As I'm already 15 minutes late, so I think of a letter from A-Z as I have attached key words in time of meditation to key letters. Suddenly I'm propelled into the centre of worship with my Lord. Just a letter when you cannot have a full bible reading can give us the strength, we need to face this day. So I go out into the day with God ever before me. Don't leave the blessing behind. God says to live simply and simply live. So be aware. I call it my three-letter routine and it keeps the truth real. I'm so glad that the truth has set me free. You can make up your own variations and it feeds the truth onto the deeper level, which we are searching for. I pray, O Lord, make it subjective. What I see objectively in what you have done for me. It jolts the realness of my faith into my day.

C, O, S...Calmness, Order and Sanity are mine today.

H, H, H... Home (where God wants me to be), Hid, and yes the devil can't get me back because God has hid me and nothing can break God's love. Home, Hid, Hinges (how intricately we are made and held)

C, C, C...Consistent, Confident and Courageous. You can live this day with blessed assurance.

P, P, P...Peace, Plans, Prosperity. God is good he will give you a good day.

S, S, S…Safe, Sealed and Sane. Despite the stress of the day don't lose your peace.

A, A, A…Awake (realise you're free), Angels (no fear) and live an A* life.

R, R, R…Real, Relationship, Rise. God is your Abba father.

S, S, S…Struggle is over, Spirit of poverty is gone, self-pity is gone.

F, F, F…Forget, Firm, Free. Make up your mind to trust God.

O, O, O…Over it, on the promises of God, order my day lord.

So these words can be said and remembered all day. Love a verbal promise as you face the temptations of the day so you make your life these words that day and experience a closer walk with God. They are like you promise to Him as He has already won the promises over your life. I can sometimes have two-hour studies but try to find the three key words I can carry into my day that the Lord has made for me. And so live the truth of my salvation in the realness of the day. Not detached but in the pulse of what my day will be. Face the reality of the day with truth and see how you overcome.

In the Celtic prayers, Monday is Joy, and so on Monday as I wake, I say the joy of the Lord is mine today. As it already won and it is over the winning is now. What a better attitude to start the week off with.

Tuesday is faith and as I wake, I think of faith, not fear. I don't need to look at the 'waves' and sink but look up at Jesus' truth. I always say 'Lord, I believe, help my un belief and the problem is over. I can drop it in the ocean of God's victory.

Wednesday is hope and I think of the fire of hope refining me and the light of hope at the end of the tunnel. Like in the Shawshank Redemption, we all, at some stage, go through a tunnel. But we can get out to the other side and know the best there is as perfect peace, so look up.

Thursday is love and there is so much love that I have received off Jesus. Like Hannah prayers of such intensity. I have crawled off my knees and felt the Lord hold me to sleep.

His love is escatonne so intrinsic, so intimate. So why try to look for it in the world. It isn't found in the world, not anywhere. So if I let God break my materialistic and selfish mindset, I will see how His love is everything the world's love is not.

Friday is the word glory and praise God, even if you don't feel like it. He loves you to love Him, to praise Him in thought, word and deed. You will get so much in return. He is worthy of my praise now weighty and honourable is His name. Do I ever realise just who my Abba (father) is and the power that raised Jesus from the dead is actually mine to claim right here, right now. Oh to glorify God with my body, as I am fearfully and wonderfully made.

Saturday is life, is to run the race and not be beset by the sins that so easily enfolds into our lives, like comfortable shoes. But to go forward, knowing I was here in this truth, this realisation all along and I use the belt of truth to hold me in shape as the vision is real.

Sunday is peace, that total peace, as I don't need to be perplexed or feel like I have got to resist it, like an exam. My faith has me whole and so pour and the glass will come, as the knowing is in the doing.

The Dictionary...

I got a new dictionary today and it spoke to me. Words of peace, love, security and happiness all held new meanings.

That the Oxford Dictionary couldn't understand.

The economy collapsed as definitions of fairness and honesty were understood by leaders.

People resigned when definitions of conscience were uttered.

People laughed and cried at hearing definitions of peace and joy.

The world suddenly seemed a lot cleaner and brighter.

Every face was shining as they understood.

That their hearts had opened

And their minds were healed

As they knew the real meanings of words had awoken their souls to life.

Letters of the Alphabet

A A A = Awake, Angels, Got an A!

H H H=Home, Held, Hinges

G G G =Gripped, Got by God, Going His Way

R R R=Rooted, Real, Rest

S S S= Separated unto Gospel, Strange fiery trials, I am a Servant

V V V=Vice grip, Victory, Valour

C C C=Crisis in will, Cords bind, sacrifice on horns of alter Conform by a Complete Change of mind

I I I= Inspired life in the Holy Spirit, so I walk out into the thing, immediate life is found, Initiative is spiritual

S S S =No more Spiritual leakage, flung out Sown for God, our own Soul's welfare

D D D= Delights of real friendship with God, Discipline in faith is freedom and liberty, Devoted to God not my Desire. Oh yes, Desires of thine heart will be yours

K K K= Know now the things that belong to my peace. Kingdom (come), Keynote (in tune with God).

S S S=Safe, Sealed, Sane, So Simply live

S S S= Stand Still, Shore, Sure and I doubt no more, a Sound mind – everything is indeed beautiful in your time

F F F=Faithful to me means I am free as I am found

R R R= Restored to beauty from ashes in my heart, mind, body, Right joy and Rest like Martha sits at His feet.

G G G= Grip of God, his best not my Good, Get up and Go, there is no safety here anymore

S S S= Sweep out Sin, Sure of Salvation, Safe in His hands

S S S =On Sunrise, road off the dimmer Switch I am Saved at last

S S S= Step off the top board, Seek now and know my Salvation and Sing a new Song

D D D= Deceived leads to disobedience, leads to Death in your spirit

R R R=Realest me, Rest in God as Root has gone
T T T= Time is now, Test not Trials, go through the Tests
P P P= Press Past the Pain into victory
H H H= Hand Held, Handmade, Hope is in God alone
S S S=Serenity, Safety, Surrender, Stay in the Secret place
S S S=I can Sit down in a Secret place Safe!
S S S= Spirit of control, giving away my Substance, I am whom I'm Supposed to be, God is my Source
L L L= Lies defeated, let go Live
B B B=Bold, Beauty Born again
R R R= Rest as remove the limits to the possible Roar of the devil is gone
S S S=Slave to righteousness, Safe in Strong hands
A A A= Attuned, Amazed, Altered, Attuned to God by the tremendous call
C C C=Crisis of my Cry to God as I Call to God with my amazed soul
S S S= Shadow of His hand under eagle wings Soar, Staying put in God
H H H= God is my Habit, strong Hand Held
S S S= Swept out Sin, Sing in ordinary days, Sigh of release
R R R =Ripe apples, sweet not sour, Ready, Rise up
D D D= Dislodged, Dismantled, Despair is over
V V V= Right value system Victory in Vision
U U U= Uncrushed, Un-damp, upside down is the right way up
A A A= Apprehend by God, Alert Arrested
S S S= Soul is at Stake, Sing Sealed
S S S= Seasoned Speech with Salt, Serene See Signs
S S S=Secret place His Scent in, Second chance
S S S= Seek, Stand, Sealed Shut!
R R R=Rules of God, Rest as Root has gone
D D D= Draw near to God, Decision time, Drain the reservoir
W W W=Weeded out by God, Won, Wow!
S S S= Stretched by God into Shape. Sure
U U U= Undiluted faith Uncovered, Unveiled

S S S=Stand up inside the hedge of Safety, unseen angels Surround me

S S S=Surf to Shore, Safe and Sane

F F F= Face white light of judgment seat, like flint, forward Looking

R R R=God has Recaptured my heart, Roving the earth to Rescue me

T T T= Emptiness filled with Truth, grip Truth, firm Truth

W W W= Worship Waiting, Work a life of expectancy

C C C= Carries me, Cares for me, a Carwash experience

P P P=Peace in the Place you have Planted me

F F F= Follow Faithfully, the Faint gleams and we will get to see His Face

S S S= Don't Squander, miracle off dimmer Switch. Sparkle

H H H=Huge new life, Honouring, Held up

S S S= Soaked up, Surfaces those things that don't belong, Separate unto Him

S S S= Scatters the darkness, God's Sounds Sustained. Surprised

P P P=Pressed just enough, Pressure on exact point!

S S S= Share Shoulders with right burdens no more, fake Substitutes

L L L= Life not Lies, Living way I do not Lie in the Lies, but Live through His name

C C C= Calling from a higher place, Closest (out of the limits), caught

C C C= Changed my clothes, Crown of victory, Crashed into God's heartbeat

S S S= Stand up inside in the Holy Spirit, bounce, take your Strides

S S S= Scruff of neck, Slave to Jesus, See the truth is real

T T T:=Black Thoughts weeded out, Thorns Tangles

P P P= Permanent worship, Power is broken, Privilege to Praise

S S S= Sudden Surprise in my Soul

S S S=securely protected in Smile of Jesus' Strength

A A A= Amazing grip of God, Apprehend awesome

C C C= Cherish, Celebrate, Conquered
G G G= Out of Grey, Goodness, Groove of life
V V V= Venture, Victory, Vision
G G G=Free of Greed, lust, Grief, Garbage
P P P= Possession of my Personality at Peace
R R R= Rightly Related, Righteousness
D D D= Discovered – Delight in the doing
R R R= Recovered Rest is Realest me
H H H= Humbleness of the Holy obedience, Home
S S S= Natural Self-turned into Spiritual by Sacrifice
W W W= Worship, Work, Wait
S S S=Sober consideration and Spiritual transformation, Saved by Grace
T T T= Held Tight, Taught, Truth
S S S= Stand under truth, Stand on promises, Stand up for Jesus
W W W=Written my name on the palm of your hand, not Waiver but look at the Waves
B B B=Best Blessings despite terrors Bought home
C C C= Cut out of my mind, Cleansed Complete, Changed my mind!
S S S= Sweated drop of blood, Sincere Sacrifice
S S S= Stay in God's Sounds on His Standards, Simply listen and hear
T T T=Touch of new, Total Transforming
S S S= Safe despite the world, Self-deny, Suffer only for Jesus
R R R= Re clothed, Related, Rightly to God
P P P=Pressed, Precious stones Person
S S S= Saturated with God's word and a new Song in new Shoes
T T T= Tricks of the devil are over only Total Truth remains
D D D= Determined, Discipline, no more Drowning
S S S= Spontaneous, Strengthened, Simply live
S S S= Same, Steadfast, Saviour
S S S= Squeezed, Sweet, Stainless
T T T= Tear up Thoughts, Terror is over

S S S= Silence is over, I hear God's Strides to Save me
D D D= No Delusions, Dropped the stick, no Doubt left
A A A= Adopted, Accepted, Abba Father
A A A=Abundantly Amazed, Abandoned to you
D D D= No Dread, just a Deep breath and Dance on the head of fear
D D D= Devil will deceive and Devour
V V V= Vividness of the Vision, never fades. Victory is the Lords

Chapter 5
A Word

Words

We hear them every day: people, computer devices and entertainment. We naturally over hear other people's conversations and sometimes don't think about what we ourselves are saying. When God uses our words for his glory, we find our words calm and soothe. There is a sense of peace when you know you have had a right thought or said a right word. We must be on our guard with our words so we don't grieve the Holy Spirit. I am amazed at the power of his living word, some of us need a nudge to remember this. We can be more than an overcomer if we cling to his words and declare them over our lives. We get close to what this must be like if we take the example of being in the theatre, fully focusing, listening to every word and having an experience. Do we have time to listen like that in the everyday chores and stresses as we rush to get the day done. What words does God hear from us? I wonder if he stares at us and sighs at our self-obsessed dialogue or self-pity moaning. We need to remind ourselves how others can hear God through us, can we relate enough to this realisation? How aware are we of the words we use and the words we think about? This chapter is about my own dictionary with God, how He translates what words in my every day can mean to me. His words of life in a limited world have saved me from mental despair and heartbreak and breaking down.

Grow Up: Meant to me to be holy, to realise I've been here all along with the truth and to have the right attitude. To finally get mature about my faith. To exercise my faith properly.

Miracle: Seeing every moments and things around me as in his plan. Each second Jesus is reaching out and holding on to us. We need to look harder to see that there are everyday miracles happening all the time.

Catfish: The worst in me that rises up and tries to destroy my sanity. But I can use even the worst of my life as God is in the business of turning it around. I do not need to give in to easily besetting sin. I do not need to self-destruct.

Prodigal: At least I'm home, I'm out of that cul-de-sac of absolute crazy actions. I'm in a jigsaw that is at last fixed. I really do not need to live in a pig sty.

Over: Just remind yourself of the blood of Christ. God's promise on the cross was that we do not have a past only a future. We died at the cross and the battle is won and the battle is the Lord's.

Hemmed: He pulls me in pretty tight at times and it can hurt but it steers me in the right direction. There are no lumbering wagons breaking up the soil of my heart. I am fenced in.

Yield: is trusting God not my basic nature? It is not a weakness and a resignation but a battle of the will decision to turn around. A yield to God's disposition alone.

Relationship: In Agappi love: God relationship is nothing short of the best only. You can't find it in the world but we all trust the substitute quick fix love thing, and not realise we have the most wonderful love of our lord and saviour.

Abundant: Is a reminder to me that really only the absolute best is real. God gives us bread not stones. He also wants us to have the best not just the good. Are we expectant for his best?

Yeast: Rise up in this new life and chuck out the old yeast of debt, fears, the past. As God says, 'Get up, rise up and eat.' Begin again.

Jesus: His name in any moment of the day can just get the right perspective back. Yes, bring it back to him as his name is higher than any name on earth.

Beauty: You are allowed to let go and live the best. You are given talents so use them. You have been given beauty not ashes so stop living in the devils lies.

Steward: I have been given a responsibility for my life for the things in my life. For all that makes my life so real. So be aware of this and call on God for wisdom to know how to take care of my life.

Name: He knows my name. Have you heard Him call you by your name? Listen. Rest in the fact God does know your name.

Liberal: Be as free and energetic with God as when you clubbed the night away. Why not trust Him and give Him that energetic best. Be reckless for God, cast your care on him. Give him your sparkle and shine.

Humble: That isn't pathetic and weak and scared but in the best of your life, and in confidence, be God humble. This means you can declare: 'With God I can.' It was such a revelation to me to find the right humbleness.

Lanced: Yep, he has cut it open and squeezed all the puss out. You're healed of all that ugly sin and shame.

Sanctified: Are you using your goody bag from God as He has already given you calmness, order and sanity so use it?

Woken: I woke up and realised the needless pain I was in when God is my best friend. And I really don't need to live the lies in the centre of my life anymore. He has broken the power of cancelled sin.

Lines: Have fallen in pleasant places. I threw my life up in the air constantly blowing plans, and friendships, and routines and family times. Yet God has let my life land in a really good place.

Thirst: Vinegar of this world won't quench it. You need to trust in the truth as our deepest needs can be overcome in God's medicine for us. Like the woman at the well, his is the only water that can take away this thirst.

Tenacious: I will not let go until you bless me. How determined are we to set our face like a flint and go up to our Jerusalem. To not give up keep believing that what God says will come true in his timing.

Locusts: All I ever wasted has been returned to me in new blessings. Your life can never be a waste as you hand over the scrunched-up dreams. He will return them whole. He will give you back the years the locusts have eaten.

Sew: The gifts can be sewn into your life like a beautiful coat, so wear it. God has sewn me back together he is the only one to make me whole.

Level: I'm safe and am above all that has dragged me down. I have come up higher. He has lifted me up with his right hand.

Knees: Just surrender your strength and do it in God's strength only. We are taller on our knees.

Abide: Stay in the Lord. Stay where your roots are so you can produce fruit in season. Stop wandering off. I abide in the vine.

Fire: God burns away the dead within me and refiners fire really makes me shine. I am gold through the furnace.

Hem: I only have to touch Him in faith and it is gone. I touch the hem of his garment.

Picture: There is a mosaic that is my life and I only have to step back from things that overwhelm me and see God's picture of me.

Security: Whatsoever things are lovely I can think on these things? I am secure in Christ he has me under the shadow of his wing until the disaster has passed.

Worship: I can stay in this attitude in the day whenever I am and despite the circumstances, I have this box of moonlight I can open anytime.

Bondage: Have I allowed the devil a grip on the function of my personality. I can leave my inner soul self in balance with my outer personality, and the Holy Spirit has a tight grip on my personality.

Sing: Yes sing into your bareness, whatever it may be.

Rainbow: Be who you are, all the promises are real and true.

Nebuchadnezzar: He was so troubled and you don't need to be so perplexed. He finally said, 'I have lifted my eyes to heaven and my understanding has returned to me.'

Alpha Omega: I am as safe as God is at the start and the end of my whole life.

Hand: I'm engraved on the palm of God's hand. I am ever before him.

Courage: I see the reality in light of the perplexity.

Athlete: Be in strict discipline. I exercise my faith. It is a real challenge sometimes.

Cares: When we feel he isn't there, he's just turned his face away so we don't see him crying with love for us. Like Joseph reunited with his brothers turned his face away to cry. God cares for us.

Tree: Do it now like Zachariah who overcame the obstacles. Turn your back, do it now. Get out that tree.

Deceived: Subtle devil tactics, beware of his game. He is a liar.

Over: The beyond has come within and risen to the above.

Yoke: His is easy and light. Wear it and don't move without it.

Vomit: It goes that quickly. All the bad in me dispelled.

God: He loves to be called names he has so many names, do you know them, do you call him by his names.

Efficacious: Capable of producing an intended result.

Non-Negotiables: Beware and do live by this standard otherwise subtly desire leads to doubt, to deception, to disobedience, to death. Death of your soul. Your sanctified will, mind, emotion are lost in desire. It feels good, it feels right. So it's Okay…is the start of disobedience

Rest: Rest, yes true Rest in your cleft and you can know rest. Rest of your life always you. Oh Lord, thank you.

Blueprint: Yes, I'm in the truest life, shape, my identity the right way round and I mean something. I am the plans that will be built.

Sanctification: An intense concentration on God's point of view, will, mind, emotion.

Heart: A person after God's own heart. A concentrated passion.

Unspiritual: Other things have a growing fascination for you.

Clouds: They are the dust of God's feet! It is me and God, others are shadows: clouds and darkness dispute the word of God and teach us to live by faith.

Go: Just get up and go. Don't be so concerned about all at home. Leave all the consequences to God, don't be in God's way.

Second chances: God is a God of the second chance.

Kiss: Keep it simple, stupid.

Renounce: Don't blunt it. Get rid of it.

Goads: Don't kick against them. They are there for your good.

Pinholes: Through which I see the face of God. They are the times I obeyed God albeit haphazardly.

Obedience: Switches on the searchlight of the reality of God.

Broken heart: From broken to purpose because it broke.

Stamped: Apply the mark of truth to everything.

Lodestar: Jesus is amazing.

Washed: The deepest part of my mind.

First love: Returned to my Jesus.

Erase: Black Thoughts.

Loosely: Hold it loosely, all that returns is for me.

Framed: Not frayed.

Bigger: How big is our God?

Sweet: In a sweet home.

Pruned: To walk again. It has been cut off me. I am not carrying the burdens and sins of the past.

Golden: Truth rings on silver bells. Apples of gold in settings of silver.

Covenant grip: Held to do marvels.

Cedar roots: Frail beauty, deepest roots.

Chains: I am a slave to freedom in Christ.

Fragrance: He overwhelms me. From deepest brokenness to fragrance.

Dislodged: Habits and memories.

Purify: holy Spirit sieves it through me and gets rid of it.

Flooded: He has flooded my life with miracles.

Ark shut: Nothing can wedge in between what God has shut.

Full pod: Flung out in whirlwind of a vision.

Crop: The fruit has come to fruition. The crop is here without locusts.

Dry bones: Do live, can live, and will live.

Gossamer: Threads of lies I believe are too weak not to break.

Excavate: I find the gold shaped me under the rubble.

Angel perfume: Feathers of hope and peace.

Abandoned: In the Lord it is meeting your vision head on.

Live: Is evil backwards. Go the right way.

Dark room: Why run around in it. Put the light on.

Pearl repent: Oyster mends itself with a pearl so I totally change my mind.

Strain: The strain is gone so has the stain.

Antibiotic: God is mine, take the medicine and get well. God has a symphony written for my life.

Zerubbabel: May I be a signet ring (Haggai 2 v23)

Cornucopia: Blessings.

Plugged: Plugged in, reconnect to wonder, love, awe.

Search lights: Searches me out of the deepest depths, deepest part of me. Lifted up out of the ordinary.

Darkness: Right kind of darkness in the shadows of his hand, I wait there.

Uproot: Replanted, not uprooted chaos anymore.

Already won: I break through to dependence.

Horns: I bind it even with chords to the horns of the altar: Bind it all there.

First love: Total return.

Leaned down: He touched me from up there!

Unlearn: Deconstruct mindsets live the more you were made for.

Zechariah: Out of the tree, reckless abandonment.

Uncrushed: Angels have bulldozed a way through.

Jeremiah: God talks to him as a man not formal, not almighty, just himself.

Windows: Of my life. I keep clean so light can pour in.

Stone: rolled away so I am certain in my uncertainty I am going the right way.

Integrity: Holds me in massive truths. I let go of rotting fear.

Tune: I tune my heart to brave music, I sing in tune with the universe. The angels and the stars sing.

Dust: Off my gifts and live the vision.

Kick: Away the rest. I am back to my right senses.

Sings: Jesus sang in Gethsemane. I can sing in tune at last.

Seeds: Sown can spread to continents. A mustard seed can become a tree.

Calvary: Get off the cross. You do not have a past only a future. You died at the cross.

God Tone: On the note of realest me. I am in tune. I can hear my symphony.

Source: God works up and through my heart.

Declutter: All sludge under my feet, thoughts of shame is cleared out. I am in a large place.

Measure: Full amount. Pressed down shaken and overflowing.

Finger prints: All over me.

Goal: I can see the goal, I have reached the centre.

Cured: To live again.

Warm: Soil of sunrise road. Gods breathing all over me.

Liquid: Gold and silver. I am liquid gold and silver poured back into shape.

Definitely: Decide.

Technicolour: Only the right colour. God has coloured my sketch. He has filled my outline with colour.

Acute: God uses my intensity. I am compelled to go on.

Intimacy: I get deeper, go into all the little things a whole lot deeper.

Crushes: Satan's head is under God's foot!

Touchstone: I can feel the truth all over me.

Cupped hands: He holds my mind.

Permanent: Experience of knowing Christ. I have learnt Christ.

Redress: Redressed out of crazy garbage and into new garments.

Controls: God's at the controls.

Grit: In the shell the grit gives the oyster it's pearl.

Untangled: God has untangled all limitations on myself. I am untangled sanity in the river that runs under his throne.

Bricks: Faith, virtue, knowledge, self-control, steadfastness, Godliness, brotherly affection, love.

Grey life: Over, now there is multicolour!

Feet: he has washed them, I am THAT special.

Blunt: Don't blunt my utmost for his highest.

Seep: No negative thoughts can seep into my life.

Lanced: God solves the problem of my mind. Cut it off at once.

Gaze: The Lord gazes on me.

Fig leaf: Don't need to hide at God's call.

Angel Kiss: Wakes me.

Sew: Sew the gifts into your life!

Blue print: Back to realest me.

Tasted: I have tasted the kindness of God.

Quake: I don't need to quake in the corner.

Constant surprise: My life is a constant surprise.

Cracked: My life has cracked open.

Esther: Beauty.

Old Patterns: Are gone.

Rock Bottom: You have to hit the rock to stand up!

Bridge: I burn the bridges I cannot go back to those ways.

Price: Don't lose it. I am bought with a price.

Belt: Belong to the belt of truth. The truth holds me in place.

Glass: Ever seen a glass cross, do we look at life through a glass cross?

Thorn: In flesh keeps me alert.

Melody: Not a half note.

Go: Live it. I must make a decision and actually get up and get on with it.

Dismount: The tiger

Vice grip: He holds me that tightly. His love is all I need to keep me safe.

Depths: Show the deeps to God.

Fingerprints: All over me.

Needless pain: he has broken the power of cancelled sin.

Shiny heart: God has washed me whiter than snow. My heart is not burdened with shame and regrets.

Desert: The arrows have fallen in a straight line. There is a river in my desert. My roots have found water

Fading: Never fading colours

Dislocated: God has healed my dislocated mind he has made it clear and straight.

Sword: It has cut off all that is not from you lord.

Cool of the day: God walked in the Garden

Fret Not: I do not need my heart to be troubled.

Rest in the cleft: this is the safest place to be. I stay in the cleft until the disaster has passed.

Meltdown: God can take away all my fears.

Unwrap: My spiritual gifts in the morning.

Application: Apply what you know.

Centre: I walk through the cross each day. I stay in the centre of Gods' will

Fountain: God has the water of life

Add on: Don't let Jesus be an add-on!

Jawbone: Used with no flesh.

Five Stones: That was all.

Concentrated: Live concentration of rules.

Scented clay: Formed beautiful.

Haunted: By God alone.

Sing: God's key note.

Gold seeds: Are in the soil of my heart.

Home: Out of the cul-de-sac. Reversed out of the limits.

Cornucopia: Abundance.

Anchored: In any storm.

Washed: Heart.

Testilisti: It is finished.

Staggering: Truth is ever so.

Enchanted: By Jesus.

Thorn: Pull those bitter thoughts out.

Cloak: The cross is wove into my cloak, my identity is in Christ.

Hinges: I am fearfully and wonderfully made.

Bottom board: Is knocked out.

False walls: Pushed over.

Husk: Is gone.

Promoted: By God!

Gethsemane: Prayer and singing with great drops of blood. I can do this.

Chaff: Can go.

Letter in a bottle: Grace sealed heart bobs on sea of sin.

Hesed: Love.

Shaken not stirred: Out of sin, still in the plan

Snatched: he has reached in and pulled out all my sin

Grafted: Branch bosom, I am grafted onto God

Haunted: By God alone.

Demolish: Self-pity.

Tower: Of safety, run in.

Illuminated Light: I live in.

Agappi: True love cuddle.

Bent: Know your bent be the realest you.

Unplugged: I am set free.

Arrows: They have fallen straight in the desert. There is no kink in my mind. I do not fear burning arrows of condemnation anymore.

Trammels: I can shake free from the trammels of the past.

Husk: The husk has gone I can recover my serenity all elbows are off me, I am back to my individuality.

Laugh; I have the laugh of the amazed.

Unravel; God has untangled and unravelled this thing.

Mirror: I align myself with the will of God.

Stones; my stones are set in fair colours.

Medicine: A cheerful heart is good medicine.

Page: Turn that page and walk away.

Arrest: I arrest and change my thoughts.

Defrosted: I defrost my strength in Gods' warmth.

Wall; The writing on the wall. I have lifted my eyes to heaven and my understanding has returned to me.

Chicken; no more chicken held down feeling.

Sea: it is thrown into the sea of forgetfulness.

Ends: It ends with me and it ends now.

Rubbish; Lord I carry out the rubbish. Rip it out of me.

Humble: With God I can.

Bands: Loose the bands that hinder the life.

Venture: Venture everything on God.

Calm: I have calmed and quieted myself.

Bow: My bow has abode in strength.

White: My white funeral day, the massive garrison truths. My release date.

Crisis: From a tremendous crisis into a supreme climb. It will spill back over into joy.

Lament: I do not need to wrestle with my thoughts.

Joy bells: The joy of the Lord is my strength.

Overmastered: I am not disobedient to the heavenly vision.

Over plus: I draw from my heavenly account.

Release: This good day is my release date.

Frostbite: No more frostbite I cultivate a delightful walk with God.

Double minded: A double-minded person is unstable in all his ways.

Time: For such a time as this.

Consolation: When anxiety was great within me your consolation brought me joy.

Exercise: I must haul myself up and exercise my faith.

Hand: Thus the Lord spoke to me with a strong hand.

Dew: No more dread, rip it out of me wash me in your dew.

Lettest: I am set free I can lie down on a pillow of peace.

Belief: Belief takes on its new character.

Lurking; No more an Abraham lurking fear of disbelief. I have dragged it into the light and it is slain.

Fly: Despite the gravity pull.

Horns: I bind it to the horns of the altar.

Log: The key log has gone, my river can flow again.

Resewn: I am only the best pieces of me put back together. That was never me.

Artist: God is the artist of my soul.

Tracks: The tracks are laid and the same power that raised Jesus from the dead pushes me forward.

SOS: God has stopped the sun for me.

Sandpaper: God has smoothed all my rough edges away.

Alabaster: My alabaster box is full of dew anointed fragrance.

Nearness: I now know the things that belong to my peace.

Furniture: God has rearranged all my mental furniture around him.

Seeds: Sow the seeds of sanity and self-confidence.

Switch: The power is switched on.

Family; I am back to my family blood name, I am established.

Fever: The fever has left me.

Deception; God has hurt me out of every deception.

Chew: Chew on Gods' words slowly and digest them.

Carry: Carry the water God will make the wine.

Uncrushed: keep the eyes of my spirit open to the risen Christ.

Rope: God's red rope runs through my life.

Whisper: It was noised he was in the house. God is my noise now. He is the right level of noise.

Unearthed: God has unearthed the lies.

Feet: today I practice the walk of the feet in the light of the vision.

Vision: I am not disobedient to the heavenly vision.

Erase: Erase black thoughts.

Rocks: I can get through this without any spiritual leakage.

River: I am untangled sanity in Gods' powerful river that runs under his throne.

Hannah: The triumphant joy of the fully committed.

Continue; I will continue in what I have learnt and become convinced of, because I know of those I learnt it.

Unsullied: beware of the retired spheres of the leasts.

Elevator; Step out the elevator in the land of your blossoms of your character. Sparkle and shine.

Enemies: When a man's ways please the Lord he makes even his enemies make peace with him.

Dynamite: may the word of God sharpen on the stone of scripture and tempered in the furnace of reality is the relevance I need.

Dye: I am out of that wash cycle.

Road markers; I have mental road markers having been there before, no more.

Latter: Oh may I build the latter end, build these last few years beautifully.

Ear: God has heard me.

Collect: I collect the treasures posted back to me.

Oyster: an oyster mends itself with a pearl.

Bush: God meet me at my burning bush, take me out of the desert.

Potential: Peter went back to his old job and was the first person Jesus found after he rose from the dead.

Unfold: unfold me beautifully like a flower opening.

Residence: God take up residence in my life as you did by saying to Zacharias 'I must abide at your house'

Vault: Vault over that thing, leap and bend all your energy.

Treasures: My treasures are posted back to me.

Rituals: Wash away the useless rituals.

Zion; You will arise and show compassion on Zion for it is time to show favour. The appointed time has come.

Reversed: I have reversed out of it.

Lean: I lean on you despite the gravity pull.

Deceived: No more deceived by wolves in sheep's clothing.

Core: Core fears go way of life come.

Compelled: Paul found such power and beauty in his relationship with Christ he felt compelled to let go, may I do the same.

Dictate: habits and fears do not dictate me. God has subdued under me all those that rose up against me.

Deeper: The water is deeper so I can swim over the boulders you do not remove.

Say So: May my say so be built on God's say so.

Border: I walk across your line of freedom from the catastrophe of the other side and see a blanket of flowers blooming.

Edge: Get away from the edge.

Frolic: May I frolic in the playpen of the laughter of the Amazed. Like Leviathan.

Fenced: No trampling wagons blasting my soul of all hope.

Broad: I am in a large place you make my feet like the feet of a deer.

Robust: I live a simple life.

Launch: I don't need to hold on by the skin of my teeth.

Met: God has met me on the other side.

Return: I turn from foolish thinking.

Stumps: My stumps can now grow and change landscapes, the River is in my Desert.

Chapter 6
Poems

Sometimes we can write a poem to figure out our intentions and our emotions and to see where our nature lies... I find, through a poem, I get to the sense of my will and then ultimately I pray with a different perspective as the poems reveal to me just what my attitude is. And my poems make me pray close to God's ear...and not my needs. I usually end up just praising Him, what is in my heart and I realign it with God's purpose.

The Corpse

I looked up and saw the eyes of God
They shine so strong and bright, I thought I would burn away,
But the rays were gentle on me...soft as lamb's wool,
They warmed and gave me strength.
They were gold and glittering all around me
I feared nothing, no one, nor anything.
But looking ahead, I saw a greyness, a grey silhouette.
My friends had no breastplate of righteousness
And no sword of truth,
They crumpled and died; all I saw were bones.
Those that stood more confident were covered in bandages.
As they conversed, they exchanged crutches,
As they spoke, the rattle was harsh and brittle.
I looked up and God was gone, but in my hand was my sword

In my heart was His love and, in my arms, were His strength.

All those I admired, been in awe of, were bandaged ugly and warped.

I touched them with the hand of God
Jesus healed them.
He dressed them in the garments I wore
As they fell on bloody knees to praise Him.

Their black teeth and swollen tongues of sin, hallowed praise to Him

He touched and healed them
They shone bright and radiant with the jewels of God
They stood strong and straight, a mighty army mustered.
Sweet breaths and shining eyes.
Strong arms and legs to run, dance and skip
To sing and scream praise into the heavens.
To skip on the rays of sunlight, climb up them nearer God
To catch the mist and feel the cloak of God
To touch the face of God in the sun.
To face Him, face to face and not to fall.
To honour and be beautiful in Him.
In His light, to dance and sing
In His love, to feel secure
In His arms to feel loved
In His hand to feel no pain, no sorrow, no nothing…
To conquer the world.

Future

There is a better path ahead for me.
The rocks are sharp and jutted but I will enjoy the climb.
There is no hope in past heights
Once climbed by dreams, let them sleep.
The new ones await, so in old age
I will have many heights to dream of in my sleep.

Again

I see the ballerina in the jewellery box
Round in endless patterns of the same
Repetition of a theme allows the ruts
To erode deeper to the coldness of the soil
Hidden treasures found in cold and dark despair
Realise there are other dances to be danced.

Moments

Oh how I long for the days of endless, windswept carelessness
Dreams were captured and withheld the reality of the day,
I floated in a world of many ideals
Each was held so closely to the reality around me.
But I loved my blindness for I imagined it was truth
Then the darkness fell on my dreams
And I could see no more.

The Past

All other selves self-flashes in a second across the older mind,
Moments of nostalgia, tender feeling re-flower for a second.
Moments of pain are re-cut, the wound so fresh and new
Moments of joy spring up, a hidden well re-found
All those feelings still so full of their prime juice.
Unquenched in a wisdom found through experience.
Will this mind remember and feel so much now it knows so much.
Or will the moments fossilise in a hard crystal shell
To be seen but never felt again.
The path trodden prepares us for the path to tread,
Pain and sorrow, happiness and love are reborn with the sun.
Its rays hold these presents out to us
Or the rain drops, them from the sky
Or the clouds of blackness mourn heavily with us.

Each day is a newness of life
And the oldness around us is altered into another hope and idea.
Hide and seek continues but the find is of greater worth each time.
To answer the question' why'? Would wipe despair away.
Acting in a response to mood, seems so irresponsible,
Awakened fearful dreams in a choking clutch,
But with knowledge of strength there is a fight,
Dark cloak of stupidity distorts the vision
Seems so worthless as the deception takes hold,
But there is a battle to be won
It belongs to mind and soul
It is fought with a hope in a dream.
Look at all those old pictures
All the smiles you smiled
Lost in the breath of the wind
The touch of persons now so far away
Their voices and eyes protrude and awaken the soul's memory.
Unfed child with doleful eyes
Yearning for familiarity of those moments
But their depths like that of the wave
Heaves its body and folds into a void in the past memory
Depositing the thought of what might have been.
All the love that is spent and wasted.
All the moments gathered into a pile, burning off heat.
Fuel to clear a void for the new.
But those moments found among the ashes are diamonds for your tree.
Pinned up high, they were good like the stars dancing, a pattern in the sea.
Or the rain dipping its toes in the ocean,
A melted snowflake but the memory is frozen for it belongs to the exact minute.
The melody of these notes frozen in their minutes create an aura and reach a height as tomorrow is awaited.

Real and True

Words of life you say on your platform in church, but on the news
Within the eyes of politicians, presidents and the like, words again
We listen more to!
Lies intently over dinner, our generation discusses.
And on the internet and email
Words created out of letters as you said 'it is done' we can, through computers, yet on truth other than making us react, feel more, do
For in death the words were life for Egyptian symbols
Carved a home for the spirits to return.
We would read a novel and believe more than the bible
The papers, His promise, your promises, religious writing unspoken
Not narrative, a word, a life is a truth is not?
How can we compare yet we make do, as so is life
In our proud decisions, we knew we believe as with aids and cancer
One day we will find a cure, even for truth
How much do we lie to ourselves in volume and ink?
And our world buckles under the structure of our truths.

On This Shore to Find another City

I keep walking on this shore and finding pearls have
Lodged themselves between my toes
Ready for a manicure, almost!
I reach down and see each is in itself so
Utterly complete
A certain part of me
That for now I lie within the sound of lapping waves so whispered
Words upon the heated sand
And let myself feel this – a moment of a dream alive!
So soon I will rise to place the pearls
Into my hands and walk
Into the city

Finding Shores

Swimming so long thrashing treading water
And then I feel the sand not even stones
So you don't need to brace yourself
To feel those sharp jabs.
A softness that even the crunch of a crab wouldn't bother you
And you can't believe it (for about a year)
And then you realise you can walk
You choose to go forward onto that shore
And so many shores after that
So within each wild, chaotic moment
Of needless pain or naked fear
There is a place to land and discover
Pure joy and safety and rest
The shore washes away and draws all that is best in.
I have dropped it all in the ocean
And now I see it in perspective.
I walk…it is only the beginning.

Utter

'And it was done'
Your words created as yet an unspoken beauty
Upon which opinion didn't lie
And no one as yet did limit its depths, cloaks of bluest blue
Hide more and in our own matter so fuelled
With H2O we hide utter truth of self
Hidden even from ourselves
Oh claw open and claim your pearl;
Then come to the surface and breathe as you swim to shore.

Stay So

I can stay so despite the fact
That there is a darkest recess of my mind
To which I banish all the shadows of my past

In the light, they sometimes show
But only behind me
What a past!
A cycle is broken in two.
To break a circle is a spiritual thing
For it shatters in more than one direction
And makes you decide
It is gone for good
Believing so is hard when you don't feel it
And the reality is more amazing than the dream of it
So I dig my toes deep into this yellow sand
And in amazed gasp at awesome grace
Which has given me the gold inside the rainbow of promises!

Scent and God

God must smell like roses, no fuchsias, no maybe the essence of frankincense
Or the deepest hearts…breathe
Does He smell, can He smell, is he a concept of smell
A smell we can't
Like the sudden impulse of laughter
Or is He a literal smell, the subtle waft as I walk past a row of roses.
Or is this the reminder that His spirit is with us to smell
Something more beautiful than words
Means…
It can only be heavenly.
I need my home to smell so, gallons indeed bunches in every room
The spirit lives so in my dwelling.

Salt and Light

A pain when rubbed into wounds so healing, cleansing I lie
In seas surges and sting dry in sunshine
Yet titillating before tequila glaze eyes over

An appetising, an appetite embraced in candle light
To live without it…never,
A pain and pleasure.
A symbol in the functions of our lives.
To feel both in doing I toss excess over my shoulder,
Yet have I lost my flavour?

On Brokenness

I didn't leave my rainbows all and be left inside this, an earthquake, to then starve
When life was re-growing above and on both sides of me,
You all call for me from behind the coldness
You make music that rushes in and drowns me in nostalgia.
Through the tears, I try to see my vision and breathe as water rises up to my chin.
Centre of earth, sounded like life, yet it is dead and cold.
Not able to be lit for long as to trust, is only a candle length burn down.
Above is sunshine, an organic in which I can change, I believe in.
So I climb out, I emerge, I am reborn.
I will not walk on glass again.
Rather, I will catch sunbeams by running over rainbows through the rain.
I choose new life
I do not need to jump through those hoops in artificial light
I find applause in the working out of my salvation.

Reaching

I cannot reach for this baton of the past you offer
For this race, I want to finish
Not up a dead end
Not in my mind
Not in a compromise of words
But in my own time

'A personal best'
Yes, what's wrong with wanting to win?
To embrace the baton of the future
Despite not knowing the map!
There is a finishing line somewhere.

In the Garden is Now Joy

Two swallows or magpies, whatever, relate such suspicions
All three orange roses
Only as tall as me
Allowed beauty
It is a place of symmetry and calmness, order and sanity, indeed.
Today is sun strong light
Out of the clouds
On me, in my waterfall beams
To ask and receive so quickly
And with friends and seeing family so knitted into the fabric of the day.
Abide in me, His timing
And I have such a stance, such a peace from His strength
As He sees the whole picture, framed!

Jesus

An impression, like a negative held up in the weakened light of dusk
And a kindness within so grows and shows
As if new baked, rising!
And yet (I say again)
So much yet to be
Yet a waiting
You stop to think of others
In a moment
An act
A gesture
A giving you're showing

So it being.
Such a different colour
The realm
The zone in which the yellow seems warm
It is (in a deceptive world!)
Yes
I do so want to believe

Clasp of Day

In the reality of the NOW
Even this second has passed.
The recurring tick of expectancy repeats
Yet time wakes us
As a minute is held in God's hand – the present precedence of love
As tick tock goes by
He stands still
Besides us.

First Snow

The first snow warms your soul
And so
The cold flakes
Melt away
But the memories stay
So is the Holy Spirit
A new faith

Oh Ye of Little Faith (Matt 14)

Why Oh Why

Then when we realise we cry
A different intonation of need
Let me please touch
Even the hem of your garment
And all along in our crippled fear

There is always a light
No, not just shining
But that we could touch, to keep us up
Hope is our reality
See…

All Those Presents

Finally opened, undusted
Noticed, taken name smudged with angel's tears
Unripped
Unmarked crisp paper, yet undusted
As the promises are brand new to you
Today as always was
Joy is your lottery win

I Couldn't Help It

I couldn't help it once I knew
I had to…without being but on the shape within the mirror
Doing what I was
But I wasn't me
Yet AM
As the glitter within the spec belongs
Although many sun's rays before
It has come on me
Indented light
So I on knees
Within the Holy Spirit sparks.

Lending Hand

Palm unread
No need indeed
What a blasphemy
I look in
A maze of exits
A puzzle of answers
An exam passed, the centre stamp
A tear drop drip of the whole world's pain

Written with the sharp point of a nail
And then all fingers and thumb press around my hand
A cocoon of strength leading me to the gates of hope
Colourful, Butterfly
Swirling on the edge of glory!

On That Road (On the Road to Emmaus)

On that road, I walk again and again
Yet the sunset is different every time
And the wind blows in many directions
I meet you, and after a while I leave
A moment's pleasure gives me ease
On that road I walk again
And see another friend indeed
With whom I talk and laugh
A moment's pleasure gives me ease.

On that road, I walk again
And in the dusk of eve
A flock of geese above
And crisp leaves blowing
Their fine skeletal frames
So intricately like waves across my path
I meet a love who is
A white deep smile of beauty
A moment's pleasure gives me ease

On that road, I walk again and see another stranger indeed
Yet in the dawns yawning of grasp of the world
I see it is myself, a shadow behind you
As the heavens pour out a scatter of gold promises
This revelation gives me ease.

On that road I walk now
And meet no other
For within my inner self's self
I have found the voice of truth's utter ease
Be still and know that I am God.

Be Transformed
>I walked through the gates of hope and what did I see
>But a thousand smiling faces looking at me
>They came up and touched my heart on my sleeve
>Souls I'd never met but predestined like me.
>And I was home.

We All Know
>We're all walking the same way
>We know it when we stop to say hi!
>We know we will one day die, never thinking about its sudden jump
>A shadowed silhouette
>We don't even move
>It has no visible strength.
>Yet it takes all, leaving a mound of earth, stone
>Patterned round with soulful faces
>And short breaths of disbelief
>But we know we knew...
>We still do!

The Seagull
>White flutter
>Gently on babies eyelids opening
>Landed by my path as I walked
>To the front office of the school
>'I've bought you your presents'
>Prayers of your mother to you
>Written this morning.
>I smiled within and let the soaring freedom live on white sails
>And I looked at the sky
>Saw the thoughts of all who love me
>As the universe's arch surrounding me with the maker
>Calling me by my name
>On the same wind
>That I breathe for life

Prayers Used

Autumn reminds me of those prayers we hear
Brown and crisp used and now scattered to the wind
To rebuild in subtle, vein like beauty in spring soil.

On Christians in a Room

A quiet meditative joy
Within all of one air, voices heard
A union in the belief
Even more real than its moment shared
And the intonations
(Yet) as we hear
Within another's words
A unique song arises to God and the angels rejoice again
Great to chat

My Heart, My Hurt

He was my gentile
He knew a Jew
My dilemma was 'love'
But what did the labels say?
I got too drunk
On old wine
That the spirit took me
To a dangerous place
Where another spirit found me
And I got drunk on
Love, is, God, is…love

Ask and you will receive

I asked for wisdom and I understood
It was in the doing
The taking hold of the making
Yes creating
That you then see so deeply
For unless the storm sprays your face (a 'light bulb' exploded: sharp)

Will you know just how wet you can get
Drip drip drop even on your nose's edge
And if the wind is cold
That you feel the ear ache shiver
So in the doing of it; Despite
And the smile within the pain
Do you climb?
Feeling is the wisdom, like sieved gold
Out of a stream
Found on the other side of the hill.

Grace

We all have dancing shoes, in grace, I pray that you will dance again

I dance in the dawn of the shore.

I've learned to walk again, the catfish has forced its way around

But it is blinded in the light.

So I lift my foot and place it high above the head that ruled in fear

I learn to walk again

Free of mindsets and other fears.

I walk as me…

For the first time, accepted in the beloved

My first love.

Father, Help

If the hour has come to make the break

Help me not to cling

Even though it feels like death to let go

Give me the inward strength of my redeemer, Jesus Christ

To lay down this bit of life on the big picture and move on into a new colour

So that I and others may be free

To take up whatever new and fuller life you have prepared for us

Now and hereafter. Amen.

Then I Learnt to Run

It cut, it bled, and it slowed me down
Yet nothing around me I thought was wrong
It made me fear the very next step
Yet nothing around me was wrong
Each step more pain, even more jabs
Yet nothing around me was wrong
Am I mad?
What am I choking on?
Invisible poison
Fear, jealousy, rage…fear, fear, fear…
Fear, fear, fear…
I walk crippled
Yet nothing around me was wrong
Struggle, strive, strained,
Horse restrained race reigns
My bit, I felt it
To add to the fear
That nothing around me was wrong.
In it despair
I reach a gate
I pushed
And I saw behind that everything was broken
So a shoreline ahead of white sand
My bleeding feet, I placed on hot grains
And ran
Everything around me…was.

All Behind

I left it all behind one day
It was finally over
I awoke metamorphosed
And didn't mind
As I'd find my way.
Transported into a galaxy where the stars were nearer
And the sun didn't burn me.
I had wings and ahead saw good things,
When I looked down, I saw

A shadow shape of what I used to be
A strange pattern pieces
That couldn't be stitched
And were colours that didn't suit me.
I realised I'd spent so long
Working things out
In the dark!
I flew away from the shadow
I looked
It didn't follow me
Attached no more
It faded.

Fully Dressed

I hear the words of the Lord
They flow full of life as silk in the wind
As the preacher cuts the words with truth
I see stitches and cloths and shape
Out of each meeting I walk
Clothed in a designer outfit
Transformed…truly.

Deceived

Oh, I have danced amongst the soft silky ribbons of touch
Not caring where the end was
And woken in a knot
Peeling from my skin
Bandages like strips
I see in the light of day are rotting
My skin is scared
And the smell is appalling
Oh take my sin and wash me whiter than snow.

Life within – Meanings within Words

To me the write is right is the right way
To me the shore is sure is safe to enjoy
To me the wait and weight has gone

For I am saved
In being set free
They may sound the same
But my dream is my reality
I am upside down and I am the right way up.

Let me Be My God Shape Shaped

May I be Paul – content despite the chaos around me?
May I be Esther – in beauty, strength and dignity?
May I be Daniel – in courage, to walk through the fires?
May I be Jeremiah – in doing, despite, so I buy the field?
May I be Joseph – in my 'no', run and my best as I am here for a reason
May I be John – on my total belief as he entered the tomb?
May I be Martha – as she listened in the right place?
May I be Abraham – as he obeyed giving God the child he adored?
May I be Jacob – as I accept the new and stop whining at the different?
May I be Moses – when he realised God is in control and not spend any more time in the desert?
May I be Elisha – who wasn't surprised at God's greatness and never limited Him?
And let me be, oh let me be, Deborah, the poet from Judges (chapter 5)
Let me be my generation's warrior (knowing the battle belongs to you)
Stronger – on – my – knees

Grow Up

Lord, you tell me to believe
Your first love has renovated me
Each layer of gross wallpaper you peel away
In my pride, 'I don't need it'
In my humbleness, 'I am weak, then I am strong'
In resentment, 'I am tired of this'
In solitude, 'I accept it'

Only then do I hear the still small voice, 'grow up'
The bare walls echo around me
So I do quietly, loudly, I praise you
In my colour.

Your Light

As sun runs through your tender threads of woven leaves
Oh the softest touch is in that light, a blanket warmth around me
And as the sun burning the edges of the golden sane, crisp so piercing
Is the reality of your love in my acceptance of your grace?
As the lights eye looks through into my room
A patterning expands through curtain veil
And your arms of love entwining me
For you wake me up
Rippling, reaching me out of heated sleep
Whenever we see light
Through glass of multi-colour
And on droplets of water
Or inside a bubble
Blown by a child at a fair
Your love is…it
Abides in me.

Building

It is in the word, no, that cement seals bricks
Of gifts given to us by the Holy Spirit.
A wall can only be built in such discipline
Not to keep (happy giant) out
But to be stronger
As fiercer is the storm as we go higher
It is our invisible wall of faith
Against which we can lean
In a world that crumbles around us
We can stand on our wall to lift others to see a better way
To rest ourselves from the gnashing below

To cling to, when hope seems to fade
We can paint it, we can live in it
If we continue to build
For it is the walls of our hearts
A place we can lay our heads down at night

Do you know who you are?

Are you the list pinned on the kitchen 'to do?'
Or the words your child shouts
Before they slam the door on their room.
Or the black swirly notes in your Filofax
Or the message left on your phone
Are you the risen Yorkshire pudding?
Or where you lost in that kiss on the lips in that film
Did someone take who you are in a look at the bar?
And tell you to be someone else as they left you
Or think you were clay to play with, when you saw him with her
How can I see me as Jesus sees me in a world where the self is
In a swirl of self and lost love?
How can I know as I know blossom moments?
That I am 'fully known' your promises of glory to me
I could not raise my eyes or open them enough to see
You alone have too much of me to embrace and celebrate
It will take an eternity to realise who I am
I? The realest me in you…entirely.

Out of Darkness

Your glory will blind me
Your truth is too bright
So I use a dimmer switch and feel comfortable
As shadows give a nice silhouette
To my old natures clash with my new
(As I still fit you into my schedules)
It is not the jarring of light as stepping out of a matinee afternoon darkness

I am used to this, for there are corners to lie in that no one sees
Yet once He does take my hand
I have to reach up to the light switch
It is so difficult (as all I have known is this)
And I don't feel well in such, after disco lights, the makeup smudged
Yet I see avenues of cul-de-sacs I walked
I ran, I danced around, round and around
But there is a road ahead
I still can't see the end
But I can see the truth in this light.

I Could Save Him

He really understands me
No one at church compares to him
We have the same sense of humour
I could save him.
His eyes and oh his lips
What can be wrong with such a feeling?
Well it was such a romantic afternoon
I could save him.
He is so very kind and he listens to the preacher
There is such good in him
We sort of let it happen
I could save him.
He loves me
What he says does make sense
We are off for the weekend
I could save him.

He says he doesn't really know anyone at church
So I think it is unfair
To make him come along
I could save him.
Who will save…you?

Alone

I am alone
Yet not lonely
I have been inside that fear
We all use the same costume hire shop
(I picked out abandoned self-pity, rejected dismissed designs, for it is a layered garment with lots of buttons, grasping hooks, and blind eyes. It so suited my figure)
I smell others sweat on it
Yet I still let it cling to me
And I dance alone
A slave to it
Until unconscious.
The empty bottle drops from my hand
Lonely is found in such moments
I'm awake, alone, is in my realisation
That I am in the wrong place
The wrong moment, for mine awaits me
I enter the lift and try to decide which button to press
As each time we stop
I cannot get out, the door opens so narrowly
Am I dreaming?
My tears carry me on a journey to my heart.
I seem to keep buoyant by whatever I find to cling to.
I reach my destination and the piece fits perfectly like a dam
The tears subside for the heartache has gone
I am not alone
For the door opens. I leap out
Into your arms.

A Sort of Woman

A sort of woman doesn't smoke yet has black tar jealousy in her heart.

A sort that smiles so sweetly, yet her mind is a newspaper of thoughts.

A sort that hugs you yet her hands itching to take what you have.

A sort that listens to you, yet has her own CD playing in her ears.
A sort that says they care yet does not offer hope.
Oh how can such duality exist and why do we dance to its tune
What is commitment or openness?
Integrity…if not in action, then words and thought
We grow through planting.

A life worth living is indeed a life that has an orchard of the incidentals
And is forever planting ahead
Fields and fields of flower heads bobbing in the wind.

This Thing on my Heel

This thing I can't shake it, its jaws lock round me
Making me utterly dependent on you
It brings a pulse to the word – trust
It makes me realise that grace
Is the glory even in it, going through it, despite it?
A battle won, so I don't need to keep crawling home from a war, I begin and end
If I just praise in thanks, the most simple of things
For when I am weak, then I am strong
So I don't keep standing in my out of date sins
Soon it has nothing to feed on
I take one step and the shadow vanishes.

Finding the Shore

To hold onto, or to fight?
He who sees with and not through the eye
When we lose props
When others are sprung on us
In a world of categories, the image
Do we live a self to a need?
(I need to be liked)

So we cling to memories and our laughs are an extension of our fears and cries.
Where is the truth of self?
For when we speak truth
It can cause remorse
How to be so much all the time for everyone
(And the prose version of poetic thought).

The Truth of the Real

How do we know what this truth is?
And if it is true even despite, so we smile back at someone who
Smiles at us
But what is it that they meant
What in life is simply true?
It is the face of a baby's giggles and that innocent face of joy that you get?
As in W. Blake's poem – so nature deals with us and takes our playthings one by one
The hand that leads us to rest so gently that we go
Knowing if we wish to go or stay
How far the unknown transcends
What we know.'
So I feel that safety is taken from us as we realise just what this world stands for
And how to play out its game
We become part of a game of new rules
And compromises and dissatisfaction
What happened to that real joy, the childish self?
The real self that could define 'games'
When we realise the fear that used to constitute the 'monster under the bed'
And we are falling into this adult version of fears
Such a dangerous path
And in the dark black decisions, the unknowingness of a soul caught in despair
In such a place
Such creativity in the poetic form can and does arise

It rises to the surface in all its splendour and colour
And it reflects in the sky
Of eternities wisdom
So is found the path less travelled.
To see with and not just through the eye
In a world of categories whose prop am I now?
What is left of me?
We crumble into this question, in our matchstick houses
Does my mind limit or expand me?
Do I take time to see the dew on the grass?
Why do I rush onto a crowded tube to then only stand still?
'I am out of the matinee and this light is real!'
'I am off the broken glass…I am a fixed jigsaw'
Are mantras we set ourselves?
And I look out at peace the world has found
It objectifies it in going clubbing
As you come out of yourself in the scene
So we can't see the 'light' our reality is Jesus and if we trust and obey than
By the light, we can see things
So we pour and hope the glass comes, trust and do
So stars shine brighter in the darkest of our skies
And by realising at last the world's contradictions that we see how blossomed is the truth
We know is indeed
Be still and know that I am God
Seek first and all those things will be added

Carved to Fly

Why do I feel so close to you yet feel so much pain
As deep jabs pierce me
You strip away my pale skin to make me see the superficial, the distorted mirrors of images
I thought were real
A touch of your hand chisels my mouth, my feet
Oh leave me in this torment
Why come and not save me?

Then on your breath
I rise and rise! Higher into the skies
I close my eyes and expect to fall
But instead I fly

Prayer

Thank you for the colours in a garden along a grey London road
Thank you for the natural glitter in a child's eye
Thank you for the sounds of birds, indeed angels
Thank you for self-control and having enough
Thank you for a dream that warms me as I wake, just before the alarm
Thank you for its reality
Thank you for contentment, despite
Thank you for surprise excitement in moments
Thank you for creating me creatively
Thank you that I've found me in you
At last

Forced Company

I sat amongst rhythms of a forced 'praise'
Echo returned in sheep's blare
And the clash of discord
Rose out of the 60s' carpet
And was an anathema to me
The dizzy colours of it all hurt my eyes
Oh take me back home
As there I walk on angel's breath
Alone.

Take the Medicine

Her plastic smile so perfectly Prozac
His calm assurance balances on anti-depressants
Her wonderful demure, sip on a small and white swallowed pill.
His, a rolled-up herb

Hers, a quick drag
　　　His, a line to snort
　　　Hers, a jab
　　　His, a fag
　　　The whole world…shiny…happy!
　　　Mine, a roll up thin sheet
　　　Mine, a smile
　　　Mine, a kind act
　　　Mine, a giving
　　　Mine, a friend
　　　Mine, a word
　　　You have given to me free
　　　Mine, only a word
　　　I look up and see
　　　I eat this miracle
　　　Is the medicine that alone is real
　　　Is that too simple to realise.

In the Library

　　　Musty dusty (cheese grater) coughs
　　　Flesh waddles past and waves lap, as pages turn
　　　A sea of words
　　　This is where here you meet me, greet me
　　　My publisher inspired
　　　Father friend: to see
　　　How my life in you
　　　Is being written
　　　To the world

Reality is New

　　　Dance on the blue with you as my reality is new
　　　Clouds moods are kicked away
　　　The whole frame is the same
　　　The biggest bluest sky, lying on my back in Central Park
　　　And in the dark, it's full of stars between which I hammock swing…rest
　　　Whole complete free, for I

Paint hope rays around the sun
Out of which I run and run
The newest blue, alive and won.
I look up at the clouds
And feel like the coffee in a cappuccino of the world
I think God drinks cappuccino cause that's where he got the idea for clouds from
And we're all swimming around in the brown stuff.

Of Him

Don't let me judge but no more 'semi students' in need of vision
Or leather jackets, beards with intensity and pain
Or clear, framed professor spectacles who make love through joint book reading
Or egotistical Christian authorities in rigid routines
Or the city type, public school attitude, so 'gay'
No! Make him free of type
And able to love wholly
With surprise and laughter
To colour and match my dot-to-dot pictures
Make him sure of truth
And make him hold me in an honest grip, with depths
Of such amazing love, that all seems possible

Live

The smile has to be now
For the next is…who knows
So digest your time
Grow fit on it
Not fat, despair
For it is yours
Not to be lost
Or given away
Or even put in the garbage
Now is you in the making
You're director, actor, all

Will you create?
Cast me!

Diamond Life Dream

I woke up within time, I can't say how
It was almost a second within a second itself
And I'd found it within such a small speck
Almost invisible
Almost just a glint on something else
Yet it was real
I could hardly realise it
It took a few moments, four in fact
To allow myself to be that real
As I'd fitted through its door
And found my life on the inside of it
What it is…I only know it's real.

Spirit – Sing – Joy

To wrap the warm
Arm's length towel
Love around her mother's
Baptised body
A dove lands
On their hearts

Christmas Feeling

It was that time, that last second never again
Caught the light in your eyes looking at me that way
Vanished into external energy of remembrance
Stop, still, still breathing yet a different air
No more exchanges of any kind, a haze, a hush, covered now

Christmas twinkles, candles burning, New Year, yet
Gone forever.

Ever Circle

    I will live this time again
    Frost will come and I will feel cold
    Again the sun on my neck
    A smile and waking in the morning
    All over again I will know
    The seasons and feel the new day
    My smile will stay on my face
    And my feet will walk that path
    Again the rain on my face
    Mascara running and waking in the night
    Now I feel the fear
    Now the dread depth of sadness
    All over again I will know
    The seasons and feel the new day
    My tears straining my face
    And my feet will walk that path
    I will live again and again and again
    Again.

Happiness True

    Freed me
    Found me
    Opened the cage and led me
    Out of the dark room
    Not a negative!
    Not a photo to develop
    But alive…living

Self-Pity
(Matthew 16 v23)

    Jesus says self-pity is of the devil
    I could think and let it stagnate around me like a pungent smell
    Erodes the mind
    Or ruse out, rise up, awake, despite
    I could let myself lie in it, deeply embedded

And fossilise
With the dead imprinted on my body
Or rise out and up, awake, despite.
I could let this moment be the defeat
The loss before the fight
Too weak to believe in anything anymore
Or I could rise up, rise out, awake, despite.

Landing

I am brokenness
Falls into the hands of love and realises being held
And pressed so strong a truth
Because of the falling.
Realise, where we are is at the centre of it all

Truth

Truth is the rainbow breath of God
On which I slide
Letting the wind tug my hair and make my eyes water
The breath is the life that travels through my bones
Without a map
And echoes in my head as it dries up the rain
And pushes the clouds back so I can see the rainbow
God holds the world like a contact lens on His finger!

Shaping

I have been caught inside my own delicate dream
Embryo floating, an acute awareness of sounds
Yet not in my reality when I am looking at you
As the life yolk.
Your eyes, I am central in them in silhouette
And the twins within the same womb, we embrace the child
Perfectly formed
This newness, making me unaware of such a tremendous love about to be born.

I Dropped It In ...Ocean

Deep pain is the sudden cold felt
When you swim in warm blue foam, and go too far
Whilst surveying a Monet like surrounds.
The moment is comforted by the pulsating rhythms of ever increasing now time
A 'now-ness' but if you stay still
You sink into the whole dark liquid blue
Cold tomb that engulfs you in a whole mass
A directory of (your) the past
The pain is felt consciously but not acknowledged subconsciously
For hope is in the backstroke towards land.

The Palette

So freely you love you so let the colours create themselves
And so they do as our lines swirl into shapes beyond our dreams
We have arrived on an untouched shore
Our footprints will be filled with titillating ocean foam
To live these moments as if a certain beautiful bird flew past
As if the dawn was never seen before
So we build a fire and let nature be
All around us...awakening dawn
We have become connected to the beyond.

Real Now

So I looked at the painting, it had taken five or six years
And it was 'perfect'
Then He ripped it down and behind it was
This perfect world
I realised the reality was more beautiful than I remembered
Than I could imagine
I was so free
No one could rip this down

So out of the tunnel of slime and all things unpleasant
Truth has set me free
And I dared to step into the real

My Perception

It isn't yours and you look at me, not seeing the aura of my heart
    I do not see yours
    Yet we breathe the same air
    Our functions are still similar
    Yet what is your world?
    What lights do you turn on?
    I want to sing
    You to talk
    I to skip
    You to walk
    Whose sun is real?
    To be not unequally yoked?

Look at Me

I look at me and you do also
And I see, so do you
We have sight but do we really see?
Isn't the world more real than the thought?
So get up and go.

Jesus

What is in a name?
How can we dare to whisper and shout its sounds?
Your name is the rainbow
A grip handle, holding the world.
It is the speckles of light in raindrops, willing us to dance
It is the truth in our hearts in the invisible warmth that
Draws a child's trust towards us in a hug.
It is life itself, the name 'Jesus' for through it
Hope rises as candy floss on a stick
To break through patterns

On quilts of guilt that do not let us rest
To delete habits that have diseased our systems
To mend perceptions
That steam up the windows of our world
I whisper the name…Jesus
And the wind carries your name
Increasing the volume
Above the eagle's wings
And the sunshine found above the rain filled clouds
Above the arch of the outer edges of the earth
Above the expanding universe
That repeats like too much washing up liquid foam
Now a song
My sounds become yours
You gaze on me and smile
I see all this in the routine of putting to bed, my four-month-old son.

Over

I trust to walk again
Not knowing how
But only one foot and then another
I am given a map by the Holy Spirit
So real like that colour shape, the glass around, so a shape inside (as a paper weight)
Can you now trust me with your message?
I, a postman, go
Will I ever put it through the door?
I leave that person waiting as if for the electric man
So ring their bell and deliver
For nothing weighs you down.

Breath

Of life it is
Yet in short gasps of fear
I give buoyancy to old matters
And it surfaces to float on the pool of peace

Tranquillity
Oh Lord, deflate my rubber ring pride and ego
A Lillo like air of self-importance
May they whizz into the end of the world
And drop off.

On the Life Not Lived

So many people spend their final days
Looking through an 'empty' photo album
Of a life they never dared to live
We have a life
Yes!
I dare to live it
Oh why not live the life
And just see what you see!

He Slept

In the storm as he said, we're going
Over to the other side
So he didn't mean under, drowned, shipwrecked
As that's what I feel
No.
He meant what he said
We will go over, never under.

It Is

And it was done, the day fell
But our laughter ran through the streets
As children squeal
Tearing across flight paths that try to define space
As seen yet chalk lines fading
It isn't the slight grin that the world spreads.
But deeper, hidden
In the last blink of a cheeky day
Seen by those still sitting on porches
Being one…rocking.
The everlasting is that planted seed

That makes us remember years on, for all time
As a moment before
So on and on it becomes the light that fills our being
As we close our eyes
In that last moment on this Earth
How light is your inside?
What lighted path of memories will take you to the beyond?
I Dance and Sing Today
In this disco inside me
Despite
Let us all be a glitter
We hardly know what we are
For the dictates confirms to us all but…
Truth.

Eight

The safety in eight
Times of touch and see
Not again to have a sudden realness oozed, crept, floated over you
IT is the Hebrew word meaning new creation
So once is over do…do once.

How I Realise

Only in the person of you is it true
The squeeze is pain free
If I let self-uncork
For in the pop out comes reddest wine
To share right there
In a world drunk on illusions and despairs.

The Plaster Cast

Around each moving hinge
So designed so intricately to do
What machine struggles to yet…?
I let the white paste harden rigid

As negative thoughts become the glue
So unmovable
I have become of my own making
Until I trust
The deep cut
Spraying a shower of crusty powder of old thoughts
It settles as memories do
I unstuck from such a firm grip
Of nostalgia and fear
That drained all my energy
A feeling my skin is not my own now…yet
New born, unpeeling the sticky feeling leaves
I walk uncertain yet I bend my knee
I am free to move
So I do.

Not You

Why
When you have such a joy of life
In games you play
Your childishness
Such a gift to cradle.
Her contradictory
Moves
Your world
Make sure the tea
Was just sweet enough,
And she would know
You'd never
Compare anything to her smile.
That she would be
Immersed
As a designer pays attention to the lining and the cut.
Oh how could anyone not want such embrace?
To not each day feel your eyes of adoration
As if the stars never slept in the day –
To know you notice what others wouldn't even think.
Or maybe she just doesn't care enough to be loved so.

Yours will be darker waters for it.
She will never know but you should realise.
Or the glitter will never spill and you will not drink of variation.
Let it be yours.

Let Go

How?
Can I have this crossword finished?
Yet only then I sought for and realised meanings not meant for me.
I see a ladybird take off so very easily
From the tip of my finger tip.
As I look up and see how gracious the clouds part to let each other through – and reveal a sandwich of blue.
How can I let go as I have seen the best bubbles fizz on the best champagne on her lips.
The sparkles within the speckles on the sea
Do not compare to her first love smile at me
I can't let such a feeling go that I have searched for all my days
The field so full of heather
As my surrender was the whitest of flags
And I am in no-man's land on Christmas Day
Irony
How can I let go of a feeling
That I first embraced
In the deepest comfort of my mother's breast
And how I can surrender, to know to be still alone
On a sea of my journey
(I am not afraid to be) but to let my oars go deliberately
How can I let go so that I willingly eat without taste
And laugh without a heartbeat
And hug with less strength
Than one brick in this wall
My prism, prison
To live this day know I'm letting go
Of the effect and its effect on me

It will be gone, it will mean I have a void
Why let go
Just so there's an echo of the letting go
A residue, residing.
How can I let go
To live when what I live to be is in the hold
Of what has left me.
How can I let go?
When it has first left me
What am I if I let go?
I will be me.

Two Years

The final journey to myself was the shortest night of the longest moment I have ever lived
And as I woke, I knew it was over.
It didn't matter anymore that I had known total, true love
For my indifference was not a limit
But an engulf of life now.
I could embrace the very best of all the memories
For rage, fear, doubt, despair, helplessness
Laid no path to my heart anymore
And all around it, blossomed the brightest of flowers
In the soil of the future
And the perfume was overwhelming

Scar (Lest I really do forget)

There is a scar
The worst unseen
That unstitches itself into my perfect world
Grace pours light into each dark room
Of thoughts long forgotten by God.
So now I need to let it unstuck, let it seem like chaos exists
For it is healed and the scabs blow away in the wind
It is the breath of God
The healer.

Stones Cry Out

God, my God, is Jehovah!
The name written within us is of such immensity
That even the stones cry out.
Nothing in this world could contain you
You hold the universe as I hold a contact lens.

I've learnt to Walk

Again, the catfish has forced its way around but is blinded in the light
So I lift my foot and place it high above the head
That ruled in…fear
I learn to walk again
Free of mindsets and other fears
I walk as…me.
For the First Time
Accepted in the beloved, my first love.
The echoes get dimmer as I do not wistfully return to the nails and fondle them
I drove them in Jesus' name.
In my own strength I try to pull them out
But they are set in
Congealed there
Oh rise and live this risen life
Bones of waste at my feet, oh leave these limits the waste
The darkness is not yours
Fly on feathers of safety in your dreams
As this dream is real.

Just to Live

I often sat, I often thought
I often queried about what ought to be.
The puzzle came upon me
Dearly, but no answer with it clearly came
So in decisions intake of breath I decided to let it be
That must be
Abided and just to live

And the jigsaw is finished.

New Old

It is the new old, nature dancing out of rhythm
As I lie here it is like having breakfast at dinner time
Oh, you say, 'wait'
I hear the still small voice and try to smile at your embrace
A greater is within me
I get up
And a subtle veil of my past wraps around me
But I do not yield.
Truth is out of, in, I mean
The dressed princess within
Would I let myself stand naked?
Would I walk down the street?
New out of old
Is your gift to me.

First Love

It is so beautiful yet you give me priceless gifts
Such tender embrace, yet yours gives me such strength
Such sweet words yet yours give me life
Such a look of love yet yours was only once
A look at me from the cross
Such care, take care.

How can I take from this Earth, an Earth that holds not your pierced hands?

For who is leading who?

New Creation

Sometimes I stick myself. Eeyore, like to the picture of my past
In a blind panic and I'm stuck
And other days I pass the picture of my past
And see the same colours are still painting my future
But how much brighter the colours in amongst the faded shades.

A Certain Sound

Why does a bird sing so sweet at 4.19am?
Outside on the thick apple blossom
Dew dawn rising, morning branch
It knows how to fly free
And a baby cries above me in concrete ceiling divide
For it knows not except it yearns to learn
Oh teach it, laws of truth
So it will fly free.

Dot to Dot

My prayers are a dot to dot.
Each day they make a different shape, each moment.
As some are answered and some fade away.
All of you lord.
My shapes fly.
So pray without ceasing.
Forever
Reforming.

Eternal Pain

Jesus on the cross is not in our time scale

It was six hours so he suffered a whole eternity of pain in six hours

And you set the boundaries and that is why the sea does not cross its line and the sky stays up

Arms outstretched; humanity defined

A Michelangelo man

You couldn't bear the human so in the Garden you cried
In the limit of this form.

It was the greatness within that was to be the victory held on a cross.

A whole generation of this world's Earth and space, its pain

Could any disciple understand?
Even in their journey of sleep
The immensity of your embrace

So did the foundations of the centre of our Earth rip in half?

The limits of ourselves as your pain was six hours of our Earth's moments

But a whole eternity within.
So you had to cry 'my God'
So we can cry 'Jehovah'
My Agappi, in such victory our voices…shout.

The Mirror

It isn't what people say
It isn't what they think
It isn't their taking hand
It isn't their charming words
It isn't their burning touch
It isn't their abrupt walk
It isn't their past regrets
It isn't their perceptions
It isn't their drowning sighs
Oh fly through the storm
It isn't the Picasso woman
The jigsaw undone
You are fearfully and wonderfully made
So live life abundantly.

My God

Oh a Hannah mother
Oh a Joseph faith
Oh a Daniel courage
Oh an Esther beauty
Oh a Noah work ethos
Oh an Elijah listening
Oh an Abraham who had to leave his family
All of you
Why you
So let me be in me, in life a life line.

Man of God

> Sweat, like blood
> Then blood
> Life blood
> Heart beating with an ache
> Loss of breath in suffocation
> And why have you deserted me?
> Your whole breath
> Breathe on me…life.

Lest I forget (The Director's cut)

> I open your word; I look in chronicles and a jigsaw of names
> Remember you have called me by name
> A pin, no.
> A camera close up on hardened scum.
> Is it the back of the prodigal son, rising out of the pig swill?
> He turns: I read the lips, tense, a cry:
> The silence is deafening to you!
> 'What am I doing here?'
> A zoom out. I see the holding out of the withered hand: it is healed
> The voice over of challenge.
> 'Get up and walk-stretch forth. Go and sin no more!'
> The sound is the tone of my heart
> I watch you, a shadow shape in the editing suite
> And feel the cuttings rise around my ankles
> Snakes like temptations
> I press play, into focus comes my life at last
> Lest I forget.
> I let the credits roll.

Integrity of Heart

> What is on your heart?
> What motivations lie within?
> Am I living within the pulse?

So a beat to remind me
Life in each second is mine.
Each heart has a voice
We try to understand its Morse code, translates, in our minds
I wish I could physically intervene, to see you only you can
Fill us with belief
As you tap, tap, tap, it is a reminder.
I hear as I listen
Your love is forever
The joy of my life
As I get closer, my heart beats faster
Draw near to God and He will draw near to you.

Written on the Heart

I couldn't believe it yet true
Lips blue stopped over
My stork carrying hope flew
You two, single solitary note sound
Green line so linear
A perfect colour against black.
No my second self-floats high above even me
Untouchable, so light, air free, yes true…alive
Then skipping lines pulls force back
Alone yet into me again
I rise up
My ruby lips smiling
The beginning.

To Possess

Surely it is not the secret of the true essence
A perfume of the heart, of wisdom
But to capture the secret of love
Yes!
Now that's a thought
That sudden or slow

That spontaneous life time
Unity of assuredly
That it is real
'I do'
To capture the secret of love, would be to discover our identity in
The reality of joy…forever
God is love.

Unexplainable Depart

I could have told you
That the world goes on
But you would want or need that
Or how I saw a sunset sky
Bleed red last night
You'd say you cried
Not for the beauty
But the sadness at the end
Even of a day.
Collar upturned as if safety entombed
By the familiar jacket
You can embrace the world again
Why face a place that rejected your dreams?
That lets time continue
For you to have to go on and on
You ask…
Once the onion is peeled, once the layers unlayered
Where is the heart of this?
This world that leaves you crying…alone.

New Friends

Magnetic energy a formula
Too complicated to learn
Or try to create
Or try too hard to make
Luck?
Chance?

Fate?
Or a great well of an ocean depth and a bird's note
Unheard of before (not found in our octave range)
Or the split-second glint on a diamond
That moment of light can't be captured
Oh no
It is enjoyed
So are you
As now you bring a better colour to my painting
As you draw out something I haven't seen before
Or add a glint to my eye or a flush to a cheek
And a rail on the path bridge on a mountain range
Step back: observe
Move forward
Interact
You add to my whole and the answer is not known
As the formula will take years to work out.

Spirit in the Wind

Spirit in the wind? Maybe.
That's why it is so full of energy
And wonder when we breathe it in
The air of the wind that is
It is full of people's spirits
Living wind in me.

Silver Moon

Oh silver moon shine bright
Yes clearer until your pure mercurial streams of light vanishes
Into its own perfection of colour
You are the hand of God
Glistening, stretched over the ocean.
The silver hand of God
Stretching forth

Gone in the morning to remind us as out of focus
Your blessings are not or ever
So do, do it now.

Lying in the Moonlight

Feed your soul with the music of the water
Feed your mind with the words of the air
Link your hands with the rhythms of the shore
As the moonlight dances over you in the rippling water of warm foam
Pulling and pushing you
To believe in the fact
It will never overflow.
Dive into the wholeness of the moon
And break the lies
Of the cold silver yolk
Soon warm as you swim
Enveloped and buoyed
You look up
And see that the moon is still whole
It is a promise never broken as you swim in a glitter of a million silver pieces, back to the shore.

Of Pain

I looked at your eyes as you cut the steak and knew a picture then of tragedy
More than an upturned Earth of exposed vulnerability in its squirming and struggling
In the broken roots of hope
More than the depths of a raging sea…so cold
It is darkness itself
More than an untranslated scream of fear in an attack
No, oh, how?
In all of this time
Of minutes and years
Across the sea of time and culture
I see your pain in the deepest quiet of your look…alone

Prayer Partner

Again, a name so dear we both love the same in value
Our salvation is a life line to my shore of paradise
Light of hope
To guide me accountable
How the cords of love can be so strong in one to one
This diamond drop of time was meant for me
A counsel with my God, through you
A vessel are you.
Oh in heaven let me see a glitter of a thousand stars on your cloak
Bathe in the love of promises and
Yes, look, yes as you have taught me to see
How great is the picture
In the phenomenal exposed colours around us
Perfect it is for us
From him through you to me
I see.

Why

I saw I thought a white dress dancing girl amidst the waves
But then the ocean curled its toes at my feet
In the sunlight ocean specks, I saw this dancing girl in sequins glittering on a ballroom floor
But a cloud covered the sun and a teardrop drip stain laid down within the ocean's pulse
Then out of the sand she arose
Kicking it high as she danced
A fury of orange and gold.
I shielded my eyes to see such perfection, vitality and life in all her twists and turns.
I crouched down to let her pass over me
But she did not.
Why is it that I saw such strength in all this creation around me?

So I put out my hand, my leg to dance
And saw the dancing girl in my own shadow…
Behind me

Loss

There is a place then I saw it above the clouds
The upside inside of them.
But today a ray of sunlight caught my face, and I looked up
To see the outside upside-down reshaped cloud now
So many pictures in the clouds
Of stories to tell, of feelings so true.
In the seeing, I feel so and my feelings take me to that place above the clouds
Every changing time.

In Despair of Love

Hope, death
Hope, love
Loved to death
Love died
Hope, why?

First Love

I my mind of flashbacks, so deep I look into the nest inside your eyes
And I see that flight taken
For the flicker of journey is in wings
And in the caught glint
I see my vision, a promise shaped so multi-coloured twinkling around grey stagnant memories.
I am drawn towards this shape
Feeling the deepest warmth floating inside a hot chocolate bubble
Found on your lips
I hear 'go and do'

But to look: it is a simple courage into the wells of blackness
Of your eyes reflecting now
A home shaped form
For I have come back to my first love
An unseen intimacy unites us
To our ever eternal being
Inside this a sky full of shooting stars
Fall down around such a friend.

Back to Find

I went back to find something I'd lost along the way
And realised it had not been what I thought it was anyway.
So I left if there, lying in the road
Repeatedly flattened, already dry bones.
I can't begin to tell you what freedom is
Unless you can fully sense the impossible becoming possible.
To be utterly changed inside and out
And to believe the best is real, a can opened without a can opener in sight.

Home

Truth, consistency, cereals, communication, kindness
Quiet togetherness
Unspoken connections
Laugher, phone calls, bread and cake smells
Books well-read and left lopsided as a telephone rings
Music sheets, layered cream crisp beds
Fresh flowers, photo frames
Notice board of activities and new menus and calendar dates
And photos capturing joy
Oh, white pianos and running hot baths, white fluffy bath towels, jokes, traditions
Celebrations
Moments so intimate, family and love and music swirling

I look consolingly
I observe silently
I ponder painfully
I reach out and turn upside down and back again
This paperweight holding my work down
Expressing a sort of living
Oh why I sigh
And type when we make things so wrong
When there is the right
To crash land and survive is the miracle of my life.

Barely knew…This is our Holy Spirit

We pick up the paintbrush
Barely knowing
The water dives into
The unseen pores
Colour rising, reacting
And an image of
What could be?
Is for formed
But it is only the water
I think.
Utterly
I see
Yet I feel overawed despite for that oh such a picture
But I have never felt the bottom of the ocean
And why doesn't the water sink or drain away?

Undoing

My head has been plasticine
A variety of multi-colour fuse box veins
All running separate
Distinct
Impact, colours meaning something
But stuck seamless (seem less) still packet image
Ribbed of furrowed brows
Still lurking, a set pattern

Yet I seem to be OK in separate acts
And only in a silent day I peel away
To lay down each separate strand
A release of stale air
Of thoughts, seen through clear and the dark
As the hidden glue binding peel plaster off
Skin sweat in sticky sweet pain
The undoing frees me to write again
My breath alone is a grace
A fingerprint touch as out of despair
A despite becomes such a reality
In window shutters banging back
Freshness enters with such a view of paint dry hope

Free from For...

It isn't until I free fall do I realise that
A structure, restricted by formula, doesn't work
It is a risk to pull the cord
To be more, to cry in the wind's face of fear
And things that look so unreal
Like a Lego land become the real
That I've been looking for
As it rushes up to me
I land in a new place and cut roll free
Am able to stand the truth for
I am one of the few people who flew through the sky
That handbag clicks around us
And my pockets bulge with the parts of the clouds that held my dreams.

My Flint Rules

A sharp stab razor
Sharp guillotine
Suddenly slices
So final a world of written chalk
Fades as those wonders
We reach out in train steam mist to reclaim

And scream to live again
Fade out, as it moves (fashion is but for a season)
And in the excess goblet shaped tear
A rainbow in the cornucopia corner of our eyes, dries
I see, in his promise, is truth
But we have to get up and go
For there is an end
And into it (outside the gold, quick fix glitter) is the beginning
Written in his blood
As only confirmed hope
Are you living half-truths?

November 5th

The fireworks would blaze and the same within my heart
As I gaze, and I would sit log lodged
To the heat intensity of your arm
Its graph so stretched over
(Depicting such highs and lows of us)
And in a tender glitter as the last speck vanishes
Our fingers so nearly embrace, a minute, microscopic touch because
Of the length of nails, is the flesh best met
Such profiles to gaze high inside the workings of the wonder, now sky high
Found wrapped in paper
Do we possess the same?
At what point will it fade?
In the universal landscapes dark cloak
Will such shadows left after catch us by their statistics web?
Or are we small enough to swim through into a space
In space to claim our own and create crackle, fizzle, dance, and glitter
Or more than?

Inside

So much withheld until
'Don't use up your snog tokens'
As if I had such will for inside
The warmth of a glass of wine
Inside your living room
(Raging fire to one side)
Inside the buzz
(They call it ambience)
Of the 'place to be'
I am seen by you, inside of me
And more is known inside
What is unseen?
As you touch that part of me
That we can never see, but where can be.
But where is wholly of the unity
As in the adding why do we subtract?
How does it all add up?
I was never good at maths!

To Hold your Name against the Grey

Can mean so much in double meanings as
I jump borders
Your side and then
Over I go.
Is it a cliff edge decision?
Didn't realise
But the bungee rope lunge pulls me back over to you
And I hold on
But every bouncing repeats
Designer labels, your name stamped, brings the only assurance
And to fight against the world
Brings such duality, as I have left the blackness and try to stay in the light
I am shown up in the grey areas
Of my human nature with you
And not against the world.

A freedom I could get
To cut the rope
Is sometimes the temptation
As I feel my soles slightly touching the soil
But realise how soiled my soul is
I rise
To fight against the grey and stay
So in the light, despite.
Branches that Bear the Most Fruit
(Are weighted near the ground)
The wind rustles through my ears, twig twisted
My hair is tangle din the ivy climbing
My eyes out of woodpecker holes seeping and the lines on my face
Run down into deepest, darkness of roots
So I hang my shoulders
No one sees where my roots meet truth
Why bother
I feel the strength draining down for no one hears my cries
To explain even what I cannot see
Yet so many blessings
To spring, seem sprung
I am weighted down into the muddy surface, despair around
And so form swaying branches and on each, I see a blessing
Sits as a bird and sings and every spring blossom bloom again.

Weeded Out

The weedy ones
Are these endless pulling out of weeds?
There has to be an end
The circle is broken, go straight, not round and round
Whose roots are so desperate and strong, let go!
It seems a worthless task
So much pulling
Out, out, to weed out

When to notice these seeds taking root?
Drop on our path and multiply
To let go of such old habits
The dried-up oldness of them
To start with a new plot as if furrowed
I am fallow now
It had to lie dormant for years
The fallow land and now
Caritizo is back
Is the new land, oh to replant
In the right place and the right way
And the right planting.

Run the Race

I saw my face contorts
As the pressure against my skin pushed me back
Into the shape of my perceived self
So small
And I pressed on pounding the ground
Shaking up all reason
Jumping the hurdle
Of family expectations at the very last minute
Leaping the hurdle of broken dreams
Trying not to slip on all of the bits
Bouncing over the hurdle of loss of vision
And then I faced the hurdle of world pleasures
And saw myself self-shape dent in its
So many times before, but now
I flew over and inside the haystack sun warm
Truth, wrapping up my old self, so making me new
So simply
Ribbon rippled won
Run the race, looking unto Jesus (James 1)

Back to the Belief

To be back in the return
As if an old friend

Such nostalgia
Yet ever new anew
As no chiding
Is as gentle as the hair numbered falling onto your shoulders as you turn back
Realising as now to not believe it is the harder thought
Struggle over
That simple is
An elation and terror 'knit jumper'

Possess the Land

Possess or be destroyed in compromise
And limitations of human schemes
So the sound effect stereo echoes of fear zone
Resounds around
It is grace
No other gods
It is to enter and possess the land
Go in.

Looking Up from the Track

It may seem I am awaiting the crack of the gun
That I can see my position and competition yet
All is darkness and shadows loom larger inside my mind
Overtaking the reality of size around me
It may seem I am listening and noticing
That my plans are in order
And all is sorted
Yet my mind is full of a down pouring of shredded paper on endless lists
To do
To be
Landing in soft loops of meaningless alphabet shapes
It may seem I am full off purpose, ready to run the race
But my mind is lying in the consequences of the choices I now unmake
It may seem I am ready and I am.

To Face
The undoing, untying, unwinding
Back to zero. Oh, oh, oh
And again to listen for the still small voice
But my mind is full of echoes, so many
It may seem that I look up and I do, from the track to go
And my mind is vice held by God
An unjumbled alphabet spells out
I will make all things new
(The gun cracks)
A thunder through the clouds
And my mind is running to bring the best home.

Everything and Nothing

When it becomes everything but there is nothing
Except the darkness inside the night
And the weight felt is the memory
Unable to lift it
You can only gaze on it
And try to touch it
Like a photo it is cold
Despite the warmth inside such a captured moment.
And you know that somehow
It will always return in a sound or colour
To that space inside, the beat of that time
That can't be switched off, so real again
For it had had its resurrection through you
And lives its life
In turning the pages of a newspaper
Its power grows and takes shape on its own shapes
Becomes a continent
Becomes the last ripples tip touch
With the mouth of the ocean becomes another universe altogether
That you can walk into
Because you have to
It is time creating
And everything now is nothing can be what it was

So that everything is possible.

Time to Look Up and Try to See

I re-find myself amongst sounds and circumstances
Where nothing is consistent except my undoing
I could end it all inside this fear
I have locked myself into a code safe
And I can't remember the numbers
Yet I am smelling the sweetly cut grass of chance and delights
The human success and love as simultaneously I help and am helped
And three people ring at once
Locked into a mind of tasteless habit of fear
I have created that has no existence
This madness cannot find a definition
In a day or night routine
Its repeat is neither for pleasure or pain
A question mark meets a question mark.
When the light comes, it is so dim
A slight chip in the armour that allows a chink in
And I bend over the tiniest speck to capture the truth
And I unlock my mind in this web fine light
Or can I?
Do I know or trust the truth in myself?
As in this light it is real
As erratic as I have been, in this space before
I watch the flight of the raven outside my window
And see blossoms on a square cut tree
And know that I can set myself free from the despair of fear
And let it all be
As the question marks erase each other
Only in the walking away
For my life in itself unlocks
The meaning as hope overtakes time.
RIP

Onto the Path Again

I talk swiftly and in one total breath of the only connect
You all nod and lift your wine glasses
It is a lonely road
I am a friend of a dear flask and blanket friend, indeed it is us two
On which I realise the truth outside of this
The OCD that drowns me in acute minutes
Where I am no more
An insanity that reaches up into all my nerve endings
A man by the telephone wires open box repair, makes me wince
It is the suggestions deeply wedged, that discord with the perfection I have been given
In my gift of life
Fears try to hold me
I do not want to stay in this padded cul-de-sac
Of fears that stop me dancing
For I have a heart that beats and needs to embrace the truth of my life
Once and for all
To live the chances is what life is meant for!

Footprints

Varying shades of dust fall in unfamiliar patterns
And criss cross my face
Perpetual pounding in rhythmic steps
Directly and at once
Some sharp rebuffs
Others vicious attacks of verbal delights
Each a cross purpose of miscommunicated wireless lines twisted
Before a repeat to unexpected ears
To think then that yours pressed into the sand
Carried me
How my tears fill the space

Before the shoreline foam wave does
My soul encased inside your footprint shaped truth
Which runs fully round to meet the beginning of the end.

Hesed (A taking you back love, and safely loved)

I tried many loves on, like a range of clothes (not even designer ones)
The sublime to the utterly ridiculous
But still led back to the truest love
A within wrapped love without labels
With such gentleness
Such depth of kindness
You led me to the light of your love
I didn't know such a light existed
And that it was for me
Always just there
I have reached out into the truth
Enveloped at last in a safe, beautiful, total love
Allowed to be the best of me
On love without a reason or need
But a telling in showing and action
A word you trust in.
Real, having tried so many types of love, all trust untied
A part of you even says:
Is this all there is?
Then shown up is the limits of love you thought were everything
Now it is nothing, compared to the first brush of the hand touch
Of this love as it finds you
And only in nudges
Guides, not pushes you back into the God perspective
No demands
No emotions
But a question: Lovest thou me?

In your awe, you only have enough breath for the essential gasp
Of yes, now, feed my sheep.

No Landing Pad

Don't let these thoughts land
No more a landing pad
It isn't a circle of round and round
Helplessly, endless, it is a straight road
So cut it out
Not like the dresses cut outs with the tags
To place on and off that childish game
Changing outfits (three in a packet)
No, not a cut out of a 'serial' on a box of cereal
No, it is a command:
Cut it out!
A real tell off rest
As truth is real and hence is flowers, cornflowers, poppies
All at the side of the road
Yes, such a calm order sanity of beauty
I gather bunches

On the Waves

And you come to me again inside this terror!
That makes me not know what it is
I have already done a once over and you test truth
Come towards me and cracked weathered face
Salt, sting, singing
It is inside the terror
In the inner parts there is that miracle
Of which you have won
A shout, louder than the cracks of thunder
Than sharply pierced lightening
Truth is that light!
It is finished
I hold you
I write your name on the palm of my hand

You belong to me.
Inside this, I ask?
Yes, it is you that stands in the miracle
As Esther stood in the field.
My love is with you in it.
And you will know the miracle of the living process
A real life, come, look up
Not at the waves
See inside this moment
I am always before and behind you
I hold you and you, yes you, can let go
It is my will
The way of living is the place of beholding
No matter what, where, how this day is
It is finished. It is now, won, now.
This is real faith
This is real patience
This is wait.
It is doing, despite
And we walk this talk on the shore arrived.

The Judas Kiss

As if tracing paper
Over, so lift and unpeel in reactions
So the second chance is given to all
Even inside such an intimate energy
A betrayal was begun
But head bowed the racing heart
Even…the world on pause.
You can turn around, yes into an embrace
(How are we kissing today?)
A detached mind or heart
When his love is seamless, passionate
He became scarred
Us healing, wholly
If only we shaped our courage and don't climb heights
If only to swing in a knotted end despair
(Relaunching habits)

Why?
Judas could have been a friend!
In that tremendous second
The universe took a sharp intake of breath
He chose, we need to do so also
Grace or consequence?

Chapter 7
Prayers

(A prayer for a disciplined Life – when there are too many demands and you take your focus off God)

1. Please Lord Help me to live my inner man, to seek you first as your slave rightly related to you, with a stamp of ownership on me. To trust in your promises and be consistent, courageous, confident to live with a burning heart full of inner strength, as the dove has returned and I can go deep and stay in your rest, back into the cleft. Oh Lord, I do not need to live a rushed life so full that it is out of control. I want to hear your still small voice and not live in impetuous chaos. I have learnt Christ. I can know you and live now, now, now. So help me live such a disciplined life. Bless me today. I ask that the Holy Spirit dwell in me and give me courage that I am through the Red Sea. I am lifted up amended and to live a risen life – in that circle so inside it that nothing can take me out of it – the truth is real. Unbelief is over. Amen. Oh Lord, help me sew golden grains in my heart that is soil now not soiled, help me weed out of that soil the thorns and briers and weeds. Please help me to see truth and let go of habits, oh that they can go way of life come. Help me also to be a sower of seeds, as behind and in front of me is the same power that raised Jesus from the dead. Oh Lord, sew together my character and that my talents take me where your character can keep me. Amen.

(A prayer when your mind is full of confusion and you see old habits creeping in)

2. Lord thank you. You send angels around us and you hold on so I can let go. I am in consistency of courage, confident and I am safe as it is written and it is finished. Oh angels, thank you that you come round my attitude to let go of fear in my mind. Lord, my mind is a place of safety. Why fight goliaths. My lines have fallen for me in pleasant places. I am out of the shadows and it is finished. Angels be with me. I stand up in who I am, allowed to be the best of me. Keeping on my level swing, risen up out of fears and doubts to stand in all areas of my life, my home and my routines, my money, my job, my look, my activities. I am in the blueprint of my existence. The map is turned the right way round as I listen to the Lord's words. Oh Lord, thank you that habits go and way of life comes. Amen.

(A prayer to not let Jesus down in what needs to be done in the day)

3. Thank you Lord, the lies are over. Lies to myself, lies made up around me. Help me today to have the right perception of life as it filters into my attitude and disposition that I stay in intimacy with you. Help me to not yield to that old disposition. I can roll and share the burden of the day. I praise you that I am strong I claim the same power that raised Jesus from the dead. You squeeze me today, you have rolled away the stones, and you have given me angels and miracles. I can live in domestic courtesy and I don't need to ever give my power away. I can let go of the past now and live. The best is real as I grow in you and strive for integrity. Your honour is my life, help me honour others appropriately as I am excellent in my pursuits and I live to glorify your name by faith and obedience. Help me maintain my relationships by discipline and everywhere I am, be at home with God and make a habit of having no habits. May my life be the simple life of a child. I just want to be stamped with God's nature and

may his blessings just come through me. Help me not to blame the devil when it is really my undisciplined nature. Help me get rid of my moods by kicking them away. I take myself by the scruff of the neck and shake myself and then do what I said I could not do. If I'm ever to be raised up, it is by the hand of God alone. Thank-you God that I have come to the limits of the possible and now you can help me. Amen.

(A prayer to keep my mind focused on how real God is)

4. Lord I stay around those that reveal your love. I am in freedom, joy and love. The rest is all in the mind. I no longer let fear blind me but I get up and do and by doing it alters my relationship with fear. I know my dream is real but I also know as I pursue my dream that fear is not going to go away, but I will keep my face like flint despite the dread trying to creep in. I use my gifts and talents. The negative old pattern is gone. Oh thank you Lord, the shadows go when the light comes on. I choose to ignore the shadows and turn on the light and see hell is so small. I move into energy, action and courage from the feelings of paralysis, helplessness and depression. I am aware of the zone of comfort because in that I make my decisions, but I must make sure that don't believe the lies that will limit or add negatively to my subconscious. I let the emotion of fear go as like a crab I lose that shell of perceptions and recognise emotions that are not real. I do not need to do that because Christ has saved me. The needless pain is me building on the sand and like the prodigal son live and continue in the pig swill. I am realising and asking 'why' as I do not need sin. Take me out of the cul-de-sac. I am through the consequences and I know the devil wants to attack the areas that God can use and in humble realisation, I realise I am strong. I now have because I ask and I take on God's purposes the sand is the world's security. I am rooted I cannot be blown away. I don't need to give God's security away. Thank you, Lord, I am shod with the feet of peace. I am accountable to you. I am consistent. I am in newness of life. Oh Lord, grip my personality, hold my mind in your hands,

use my talents for you alone and May I claim victory over any strongholds. I know I pray to a God who holds the third space. There is no end to the galaxy and you hold it like we hold a contact lens on our finger. I tattoo Isaiah 40 in my heart as I realign my mind. I am indeed the finished jigsaw on top of the box, not the chaos of bits tumbling around inside. I do not need to be out of sorts with myself. I am in a palace, not a pigsty, because you did die once and for all on the cross and had to call him God, not Jehovah, and now you are with me and you are in heaven and it is real. It is the invisible, the intimacy is strong. I take my very next step with you Lord. Amen.

(A prayer not to be diverted from the truth by being influenced by others)

5. Lord, I am so grateful that you have revealed so much to me and at least I pray that I stay away from my old nature to be so sorted, to keep on keeping on and believing this vision and me on the shore. Please don't let the invisible thoughts of lies spoken over me by any family and friends limit me. Please take away, prune and peel away wrong perceptions and old dispositions and anyone who would take away my first love. May I walk in newness of life with my new nature and my walk be in step with you. Help me to stay away from the past and negative thoughts and attitudes and friends who are no good for my walk with you. I knew your butterfly kisses are real and genuine and not underlined with anything. Oh, I want to stay in the right attitude and the risen life so I live my days full of hope. I pay the price Lord, I live out the vision not the lusts of my flesh. Oh Lord, I do not pray for an easy life but to be stronger. Amen.

(A prayer of expectancy)

6. I do not pray for tasks equal to my powers but powers equal to the task. Oh Lord, help me connect every thought like clothes hooks onto a clothes line with the thoughts of God. Help my thoughts be in line with your will. I'm in my God

shape. I do not need to live out sin in my life. I don't need to binge or freak out but I can remain in the vine. There is no need for sin at all. It is not even that I shouldn't sin but I just don't need to at all. Oh help me write my vision and love the right vision. I am pressed like Mary who had seven demons pulled out! You indeed call me by name and alone is your intimate tough. May I pray the intensity of prayer like a Hannah, may I know your voice like Mary did in the Garden. May I know your touch like Thomas did, the indescribably precious touch of my Lord my God? Like Peter, how you restore us in private and then before others. Oh yes, I do love you. Thank you for my journey with you, my hands on the plough, face towards Jerusalem, once again returning to you. Thank you that once again you know me. Amen.

(A prayer that I overcome and learn Gods' ways)

7. Lord, thank you that your name overcomes all patterns of my disposition. I surrender my old disposition to you as you have emancipated me out into personality and sewn me rightly together. All my best bits, sewn together. All this temptation happens to everyone and I 'm so glad you can break the circle that tries to bind me, to limit me to those things and make me leave the shape I was made to be. Help me not be something else in an excuse driven by a fear that like an invisible gas permeated my thoughts and solidified them actions that would shame you. Help me know that temptation yielded to is indeed lust deified. I don't want to panic and have fear and timidity turn into raging pride and idolatry of self. We are going to be tempted (that Lord, I know is not the sin) but Lord may I leave alone now the temptations themselves I have no business to suffer. Help me Lord to climb higher and as I face the right temptations for the plan of my life on your level, may I reach higher up to your ways and obey. I know the temptations I encounter link to the type of personality I possess. Lord, may I set the right thermometer setting so I know your secure me in the midst of my temptations (Heb 2 v18) and I know then, like that game

played as a child, if I'm in too hot or too cold a situation. May my inner man temperature recognise, read and register so I am able to go higher into your walk for me that I can walk before you and be holy. Amen.

(A prayer for victory)

8. Lord, please go into that place in my mind where feelings of fulfilled promises are trapped and set me free to do your will. Help me apply the truth that love has set me free. Help me use my gifts for you and work out the fruits of love for self-discipline and of a sound mind. May I be like David (from the bible) in my life time and have domestic courtesy with all I do? May I be aware of Jesus, angels and miracles colouring my day? I am allowed like Queen Esther in the Bible, her beauty; but not to be too obsessed with myself. Oh Lord, my conscious life is but a tiny bit of my personality but Lord may I take care of it. For you Lord look after the unconscious part I know nothing of but may I guard with all I have, the conscious part of my life of which I am responsible. Amen.

(A prayer to be free)

9. Lord, it is in the everyday may I be just so rightly related to you so that it is your discernments, not my emotional evolvement, that comes through to bless another soul. May my own sympathies not block the way for what you truly want to do with another, be they friend or family? Lord, may I be conscious of my walk with you and how I conduct myself and also realise I do this by being consciously dependent on you, not on trying to be a good Christian. I know I try to be holy but Lord, may I just be faithful in human life as it actually is. I try to aim and be successful in my walk with you but Lord, may I just manifest the glory of God in my human life that Christ indeed is hid in my life in the centre of all my human conditions. Lord, I want to win into freedom. I don't need to suffer from wandering thoughts or anything. I do not need to live needlessly, let me shed my individuality

oh Lord and be truly emancipated out into personality. May the devil have no grip on my personality? Jesus death has broken my individuality and united my personality with the Lord's. I am free, so free on the inside. Oh Lord, help me to see me as you see me – to hear your call as one with the nature of the sea in him, to preach the thoughts of God, never the experience. Like the prodigal son, I realise that I can get up and not stay in the pig swill. I am suddenly awake and a realisation hits me, oh what have I done. May I be haunted by you alone Lord. Help my strength to be in you alone, Lord, to stay in domestic courtesy, not lose it in the wrong temperament. I believe I can live in peace, despite the world's pressures that impose such demands and expectations. Oh Lord, prove thy consciousness in me as I rest in the cleft once over, do it, think no more on it (no more moronic!). I will sing in these ordinary days, Lord, and I will listen to my God and not my fears. I keep my hands on the plough and I live in the power of your love, the Escatonne, charismata, and Caritizo of love. I realise what it cost you to forgive me Lord and I stay held in that vice, so, so constrained by the love of God. Amen.

(A prayer to stay in shape)

10. Dear Lord, thank you that my real life has started. I am like liquid gold and silver. The vision of that 5-year-old Cyprus girl going through the vines into shape. I knew you had called me. I have been tested. I am out of the hurricane of my whole past with my crumbled vision and I venture with you. Lord I am available and send me as I am apprehended by you. Now is my time. I am in the shape you gave me moulded by you. Help me be the realist me, Lord as the reservoir drains, I am left in freshwater. Your name fills me with worship and awe. It is like a domino effect as I step out and obey you I see my landscape change. I am awake in the truth of non-negotiable. I have come out of the shadows. I am out of the matinee into the real light. Habits were the rewind of a film. I am now at the end of it and you have acknowledged and named me. Oh Lord, it is over, it is finished. I am the orange rose in the garden of sanity. I can let go. I am free. I

am lanced. Oh Lord, see the art in me. I know I now have nothing to fear. The strong light is on so I don't need to run around in a dark room – the only vice is the vice grip of love. I have everything appertaining to life. I am so much more beautiful than the roses. I am alive and in you is so easy to live. I use my gifts of happiness and beauty each day. I do consistency have courage, confidence for faith not fear in me and work is to do. Help me Lord to just believe. I do not have to doubt and thrust my hands in your pierced side. Oh Lord, Jesus you had to leave your father and be separated from him so that we don't have to. We always have our Jehovah, our Agape. Oh may I be holy and set apart for you Lord. Thank you that whatever happens here, I am not home yet and one day I will be in heaven with you. Your tone create the music oh God. Amen.

(A prayer to be of use by you Lord)

11. Thank you – I can never praise you enough. You have planted all my seeds of hope and they can blossom and change the landscape of my stance, attitude, perception and disposition. I am indeed changed. All of us get grace but how many of us go through such skilful cutting and produce the gemstones that are set by you. You Lord can set us ablaze. Oh those, Lord, that respond to the heavenly vision we have gemstones, as all these years finally the rest is cut away. May we shine for you? How many of us let you cut 'that' away, for good; shedding identity to find their personality in you. I'm so glad I did finally surrender and I can see the truth. That you have finally bought me home, that only in you is all I build, not swept away. That blessings like the cornucopia, the horn of plenty is mine. That sins grip on me is done away with. I am in the hands of God. I wrestled with the angel and have changed my name. I am a woman of faith. Lord, thank you that your guidance has been a gentle pushing, nudging, not a shove. Thank you that you gave me time to repent and you waited for me and I can be confident about tomorrow as I walk with God today. I unlearn the lies and I live in the spirit of love, power, discipline and a sound mind, not a spirit of fear.

There isn't one! Like the turtle dove, I am at peace settled and single minded. I am in childlike trust restored with you. As I came across the expanse of the vision, you create the harbour and I can come home. I pour and the glass comes. There is better to come. The best is yet to be. I now seek you see, you and I let the gemstones pour over the blossoming land. Amen.

(A prayer for clarity)

12. Thank you my saviour, you are not a God of disorder but of peace. You send your breath like gales in summer sunshine breeze through my mind, spreading truth. All I was is now nailed on the cross as I crash softly into the heart beat of God in his Hesed love. I am now a woman of faith, the stones of mindsets and pride and individuality have been rolled away, habits go, way of life comes. I exercise my faith. I walk through the Red Sea. Jesus has sweated blood in Gethsemane for me and because of this, I belong to my peace. I have come back to my right senses. I was here all along and Lord, thank you. You helped me decide definitely about sin and I let go so the full life can come. Identify me with your death until I know the suppositions are dead in me. Oh take the desperation of my sin that lusts against the spirit of God and identify me with Christ in childlike wonder. Oh my bridges are burned oh Lord. My nets are mended and I can throw them on the other side. Oh Lord, I pray I stay so close to dedicated words on the higher ground despite the grey of the day. I am now getting used to the real after being in the matinee darkness. Now I can see the real light as shadows go and I make sense of it all. Lord, help me to wait in the inspiration of my vision. I get out of the box of limitations and attack evil with truth. I balance my inner soul's self with my outer personality. Help me stay round those who show me who I really am. I ask for the other half of the blessing. I invite you in oh Lord. I am intimate with you alone. Lord, prove thy consciousness is in me today. I give up the right to myself. I am emancipated out into personality. Thank you, your promises are real, available, essential and unlimited and I go higher as I see more truths revealed to me. I keep these truths

safe and deliberately leave sin alone. Lord, make me so aware of who I let into my inner circle. You truly nailed my sin to the cross. Oh may I yield my disposition that rules where the Holy Spirit's peace should be. Take my might have been, Lord and please make our future. I belong to my peace at last. I do not call my ignorance innocence and then call my innocence purity! Amen.

(A prayer for grace)

13. Lord, I am on Mt. Zion, the place of grace. I am no more on Mt. Sinai under law and in the limits of self. I am whole again. I leave the rest alone, no doubt, no debate, my dreams are real. I am in a spirit filled life. All my pieces are put together and fit perfectly. My miracle is that I am restored. I have gotten back the years the locusts have eaten. Oh cleanse my spirit Lord, so it is not paralysed. Help my spirit to ever look to the risen Christ. May I live higher in the insight of my character and in my personal character? I have climbed to the top and the view is my future, my hope. Lord, up here this high, I am lifted. My soul is lifted and your sound is my sound is my life. May the mind of my spirit be in agreement with God? Here on Mt. Zion. Lord, I belong to my peace – I come up higher to Jesus, not to what I feel. My identity is in your value system. I live simply and simply live and kick away out of date habits. Oh Lord, you indeed have me by the scruff of the neck. Here on Mt. Zion, I stay free of distraction. I live in disciplined vision so protected by the power that raised Jesus from the dead. The pillars of fire and cloud remind me Lord Oh Lord, that you are the first and last so I am hemmed in on a safety chord, always held. I come up higher, not to what I feel but where I belong. Oh Lord, help me to work out what has been worked in me. I am here. The climb step by step is up and not round and round the mountain. A few steps after, going round the mountain for years, a few steps up higher and I am home. I come up higher and I am home. Amen.

(A prayer to stay free from the past)

14. I at last give God a chance! I came apart not in the world's collapse definition of falling apart! But actually come into my Lord's place for me. I step out of and into I have unlearnt so much, I now know what not to yield can mean. Oh Lord, help my unbelief. I can now give the very last of self. I truly, truly surrender. I have found you in the quiet of the desert where the expanse of the vision can be truly seen and now I can go as lines have fallen for me in pleasant places. I find my wells. The Red Sea means stone of mindset rolled away, habits are out of my mind. I have walked through my Red Sea. I am in the living way allowed to be fixed like a fishing net, i am not full of knots and tangles. To live entirely for you I have thrown my nets on the other side. May I stay in that relationship with you Lord. Just one touch and I am hem healed. The kink taken out of my mind and the arrows of victory and fallen straight and aim and hit the mark. Thank you for this way of living way. Hooks are gone and I am free. Oh Lord, help me to stay in the place of beholding for if I am in your will, then it does not matter what or where I am. Oh Lord, hope deferred maketh the heart sick and my heart is restless till it finds its rest in you. I am here all along. The deep calls to deep, the diamond is in my hands. Oh Lord, I am Esther beauty for such a time as this and God makes Ark-shutting decisions. I am in the living way, despite the grey of the ordinary, God is always here and I sing in the ordinary days. I have got up and gone where there was no safety anymore. No more elephant strength only gossamer threads remain and cannot hold me. I know in all I do, God's honour is at stake. I am re-hung like a framed painting in the promise of land of your household. The chaos is no longer bigger than me in the storm. I do not blame God for being the terror as he is my peace. I live in him, not the situation, and I am safe. I am on the chaos in his Ark. It is no longer bigger than me. Oh the Lord has bought my mind home. Oh how I need thee Lord. I am re-rooted, not the upturned soil all wriggly and helpless. I am now planted safe and securely. My heart has been washed like Paul on the Damascus road. I am given sight and

I am the nature of the realest me. For such a time as this, I do not squander the miracle that is my life and truth is off the dimmer switch. What a year. I am now the right way up, looking up. Amen.

(A prayer to rest in the cleft)

15. Thank you Lord that I love your law and nothing can cause me to stumble. I do not need black thoughts. I can erase them with the grace rubber.' I do not need to live in a confused chaos. I am satisfied that you as X are indeed the answer. You are next to me. I can rest in you. I can be who I really am. Oh Lord, order my steps that all the steps I take today are in the footprint shape of rest, renewed and restored. That I am indeed plugged into the right socket, that my power comes from you, my only source. Lord, may I drop habits immediately. May I feel the sting burn of wrong of what is not good for me, that I stop gripping hold of wrong and let go so full life can come. Lord, you alone have bought my will, mind and emotions right back to their blueprint true self. That only in your am I the right shape, that the freshness I feel is the right adrenaline. That when I go to church, it is with more enthusiasm than a night out. That I am as excited and beautiful for Jesus on his day as I am getting all dressed up. I pray that I live as a sanctified soul. That sovereign, Lord, you alone have made me so lovely that I am cut and implanted with order, sanity, holiness, that I am in my God shape best performed flowers. I pray that I blossom in soil minus the weeds of strongholds and like butterflies that thoughts and words may land on my beauty in you and fly away. I just so let go of subtle thoughts that take away the realest me. Your perfume, your nearness give my clay shape scent. Oh my aim, Lord, is to be near you today. I am perfumed clay. Please protect me that I am not deceived. Help me to be aware and know no other spirits of fear can get me as I am in your power love, and I am of a sound mind. Habits go, oh Lord and way of life come. Amen.

(A prayer to be a woman after God's own heart)

16. Oh Lord, may I be a woman of substance and such a woman of God that the impression of God be in me. May I shine brightly? The light bright my wick trimmed so my light can burn steadily. I am allowed to develop the beauty of God so I look after myself. My windows clean so your light can shine through. People need to see Jesus in me. Break the oil reserves so the golden oil of blessing can pour. I am indeed at my burning bush after all these years. God has met me and knows me. I do not need to live any unnecessary friction. I let go of the unnecessary and meet you. You meet me where I am. My nerves, mind and heart don't need to be spent out and crushed. I can indeed erase the black thoughts. Help me to be worthy of the life you called me to lead and pour and do as you are my future and stop going round the mountain of repetitive habits that just cause me confusion. Thank you that I can act and react in the light. Knowing I remain in the vine. I am grafted in so I don't need to react in chaos as I realise my character in being a branch of the vine. Oh Lord, may I now live the non-negotiable awake in my vision. I am home in safety and rest, and in the right fellowship. Oh Lord, thank you that you have kicked down false walls. That you crush the head of any additions and passions that would destroy us. May I stay always on the right warm soil, sunrise road reaching over for my destination that is heaven, with my hands on the plough, going the right way? The productive way with the right results, events and people. Oh Lord, I never need to look back as I now live through the trials and just do not touch the temptations as the trials do create the realist me, in Jesus my Lord. Amen.

(A prayer to help my unbelief)

17. Lord Jesus, help me just to believe. Yes I am out of the tree. I'm home and healed. I'm like the lame man I finally just got into the pool. Oh Lord, I give you my all and only what is in your favour will be in my life. Whoever, whatever it is. I take Isaiah 61 v7. I speak and I believe instead of my

shame, my portion will be doubled and instead of disgrace, I will rejoice in my inheritance and in this time I will receive a double portion in this my land, that your plan is worked out and I never need to lose my peace. My joy will be everlasting. I am an eagle (I can soar on eagle's wings), I am not a chicken (charging around not knowing where I am going.). I rest as you rested your head. It is finished. Bless the ministries out there who commit to you. Help me to stay healed from the inside out, burn my lips Lord. I am out of the pit. Help me to grow up. John 17 v4. I have bought you glory on Earth by completing the work you gave me to do. Help me to honour you with all my abilities. I am repositioned. Oh Lord, I climb the rungs of the ladder, I do not need to stay in this manky well and your word is the only way home, not left into fears or right into addictions but rung by rung straight ahead and I never need to lose my peace. Amen.

(A prayer for when I lose my courage)

18. Thank you Lord, you are changing the steps (the rhythm) at work, in my family in all my ways and my attitudes. I can now I dance in harmony as I am released in all the actions I do each day. I do not need to be afraid of sudden terrors, that you keep my foot from being caught. I do not now have liquid cement around me that hardens throughout the day. It is the certainty of protection from you. I am out of the Hoover's vacuum bag. I do not need to let the world suck all the life out of me. I am not part of the leftovers. I now stand on the corner stone. Oh Lord, may I dance in the depth, width and length of your salvation and stay in the desert flower with the deepest roots. I am not attracted to the allure of passing glitter – but I stay in the cleft of the rock. I am on my moral frontier, surveying the new land of milk and honey, and seeing, indeed, a river through my desert. Oh rock of ages, on frontier cleft for me. That my nets are filled with sweet surprised, that the roadblocks are gone. Oh may my will, mind and emotions stay harnessed to heaven, my face up to Jerusalem fixed in vision and voice. I am in my fulfilled destiny and I realise I live in a palace, not a pigsty. Please give

your angels charge over me and that I realise I am freer than a non-Christian, that my fears are handcuffed. God, can do it, it is Him alone. I can call on Him and they can't. (Deut 8v2) Oh Lord, may I never forget what you did leading me through my desert these 40 years. Oh humble me again today. Oh test me and see what is in my heart. Oh Lord, you have airlifted me in the floodlights, have searched and found me and I am saved. Being a Christian means all is in chains, that the devil is a liar and doesn't want me to see this. Oh Lord, you don't break me, you make me and I am the realest me in you. Amen.

(A prayer to recognise I belong to the Lord)

19. Oh Lord, you have moved into my heart and switched it on. I call out, I cry out that you would bring all of me into the light so you can guard all of me through faith. Safe and free in the centre of your will is the only life worth living. Oh Lord, only if you favour it, please show me your favour as I walk in faith with gold bones and perfumed clay, body and soul transformed by your beauty. I walk only in faith and each step if it's in your favour can be a miracle day, and the same glory that is yours is mine. Hence, I honour my mind and body. I dress in your wardrobe in quiet strength and discipline content in the vision shape. Oh battered and out of ordinary days out of the valley into the Holy Hill (Prov 4 v18). I can exclaim with a Moses shiny face, the same power that raised Jesus from the dead. I claim today. Oh Lord, may I be filled with first fruits according to your greatness, that my stump will grow to a tree and change landscapes (John 12 v24) that I am safe in the desert flower cleft and I can sing in the ordinary days. I know now that you promise me you will in no wise, fail me. I pray for wisdom, love, fellowship, safety and joy on this moral frontier. Thank you. My value from birth has not changed, may my words be liquid gold and silver. I rearrange my mental furniture around you. Lord, please help me to form the right relationships and don't let the devil either puff me up with pride or bring me down with fear. Amen.

(A prayer to claim my victory in Christ)

20. Oh Lord, I take the deepest spiritual breath of peace and sing in tune with God's note. I pray he is the noise in my home and mind. The universe sings. The stars sing. I pray I live in his tune because unlike the world his tune is the right level of noise. I can blossom in the best. I pray I discipline myself in my stance, attitude and perception. On how I look at the creation around me and grow into who I should be. I stay in my God shape at the right train station to pick up the vision. The vine is my only root that I am attached to so only in Jesus can I do all things. I stand up inside. Oh Lord, thank you, my weeds have turned to cornflowers as I seek you, that you alone take the grey areas. Help me to build real love. Oh Lord, all is behind me. May I never forget your word endures forever (Matt 25 v10). My oil is ready and the Ark shut door, is shut, it is finished. I am aggressive only for you now in Angel grip fear, only with respect submission to God. I am back to my blueprint with truth hands that hold up, the whole of heaven my heavenly birth right is behind me to win the battle. The battle on the moral frontier is the Lord's and I am His. Amen.

(A prayer of knowing my identity in Christ)

21. Oh Lord, I am out of my drowned stagnant life and into green pastures. May I live a testimony led life and go the narrow way, stamped so 'post me' where you want me to go. Thank you. My hinges are healed and I am taken into a land in which I shall lack nothing that torrents are released and my dams have burst. Thank you that you have stepped into my history and taken away my wrinkles that I now live cut off the right bat that I am Technicolour from black and white as you call me. Break the lies over me oh Lord and make me whole. Thank-you Lord. Your sword is drawn on my behalf. May I walk before you and be perfect (Genesis 17 v1) that you have drawn my God shaped outline and now you fill it with colour.

Oh habits do indeed as way of life comes. I reclaim my song of peace with thanks and praise and stay that near to you. Oh Lord, I step up into a new dream from black sin, red blood/sweat into Gethsemane into free white like the white pages I write on. Oh to be so in tune with God's keynote (Psalm 90 v11-12) for who knows the power of your anger. Lord, for your wrath is as great as the fear that is due to you. Teach me Lord to number my days all right, that I may gain a heart of wisdom on dry land. The strain is over and I am through the Red Sea as you met me on dry land at the end of myself is purified hope. I Come out of the Ark, shut led decisions on dry land and bring my seeds which I plant where there was devastation. Oh Lord, lest I forget! Amen.

(A prayer to know you fight for me Lord)

22. Lord, may my talents for you take me where your character can hold me. May I always know that I am whole in my identity so nothing gets in. I deliberately turn my imagination to God and live in personal holiness that my talent and character blend and are whole. Help me to take hold of the miracle, not the way out! To live in victorious dwelling, walking after the Holy Spirit that I indeed change direction to remember whatever my spirit 'orders, my soul has to pay for it. Oh Lord, you have indeed moved into my heart and switched it on. Please correct and redirect my emotions, appetites and attitude that I live the Jabez lifestyle in my parade, my palace. Teach me your ways, show me your glory, cleanse and free and embrace my soul, Lord, with the blood of Christ that I don't need to go below that line. I can stand up in the middle of everything, every day now I know the light, how much darker is the darkness. Help me bring glory to you on Earth by completing the work you gave me to do (John 7 v12) and restore me the joy of thy salvation and sustain me with a willing spirit (Ps 51 v12). I am stood up by Jesus out of the cattle feed and free from the devil's grip on my personality, no more scarlet woman. The fire place is central to myself in the right place. My home of self is not out of control it is steady and consistent. The stump of the tree is still

there it can grow again. My nets are full of vice held love not lies. Oh as I seek you first Lord, I can see what you can do. Please do not hold your favour from me. I dance now in the sunshine. May I not be deceived for when desire is conceived it gives birth to sin and sin when it is full grown brings forth death I am the lords.

23. Oh dear Lord may I give you your love not try to find it or give it to any friend or family or expect such love from them when only your perfect love fulfils. Oh please make me discerning to actually listen to you and have the courage and determination to act on what you tell me. Make me patient and let your will be done. So please take the reins so I do not do it in my own strength. Help me to keep hold of and use the open presents of your grace and to remember lest I so often forget the picture of truth I live by now. Oh I have truly learnt so much especially self control, discipline, perseverance. It has produced character in me. Do not let the strongholds or mind sets of despair build up in me. Help me to obey your word and resist the devil and he has to flee. Thank-you, the victory is already won, you have slain my Goliath you have given me the desires of my heart. help me to walk uprightly and have your wisdom. Please make me wise and to be in the right relationships and not lose the opportunities you give to me in who I am meant to be in you. As a Christian, I can live a victorious life over the flesh and the devil. Thank you. I can call on the Holy Spirit as he intervened for you even in Gethsemane. Make me so wise of your life and the Bible that my words will come from a heart soaked in love for you and penetrate the hearts of others. Like Jeremiah, I just buy the field. Now my Goliath is gone, I have inner victory. Thank you. From today, I walk in newness, wholeness, completeness and the future you destined for me. Amen.

(A prayer of healing)

24. Oh Lord, may I stay with my first love despite living in this fallen world where everything around us seems to work against us. I pray that I continue forming an intimacy with you

Lord. May I not be so distracted from my first love and not lose sight of what is truly important? May I never fall out of love with Jesus? Lord, may I recognise you look at the heart and I can be intelligent, even gifted, yet is that deep walk with you that you long for. Can I go deeper Lord? May I discipline myself so that I draw near and abide with you alone on that deepest level? May I be still and know that you are God that in my solitude I cultivate serenity. That in my surrender I let go. Help me hear, trust and obey your voice and not erect strongholds but simply take your hand and obey. Lord, may I live in your strength and your wisdom that I keep God at the centre and not walk on the broken glass of my life again. Oh Lord, may I live in the reality of what you have already done for me. Lord, I dwell in the vibrant awareness of your nearness. May the pace and shape of my life not strangle the relationship I have with you. You have given me such harmony within that I can indeed live with my inwards desires and my outward life that I take the time to know the joy of accomplishment, that I may be single hearted and in crystal clear simplicity. Lord, may my heart not be fragmented that I may dwell in peace of real relationships, of warm hugs, laughter, quiet walks and talks. Lord, may I recognise the balance and control that I have in my life and may I reorder my life around nourishing priorities that I will live life in sync with what truly matters. That I can make my life a series of deliberate decision strung together with a strong thread of purpose that it is not a clutter and that God, the priceless pearl can be found among my scattered beads. May I recognise the richness of silence and the opportunity it creates? Oh Lord, you are more deeply at work in my life than I could ever imagine. That in you, I can claim an inner safety and a calm sanity. I can judge myself kindly, recall the meaning of my unique call, reacquaint myself with my dreams and filter out the non-essentials. Oh Lord, I want to get to the core of my life as you are waiting at the core. The silence helps define the significance of the sound. Oh Lord, may I drop all the wrong luggage so my hands are free to embrace all you have to offer me. Lord, may I submit out of love so it is a strength and not out of fear, which is a weakness. Lord, call can be turned around for my good. That your timing is indeed perfect. I do not need to do it on my own anymore, Lord, but in the Lord's strength. Oh Lord, you have made straight what I made crooked. Amen.

(A prayer that I live my new life in Christ)

25. Lord, help me maintain my relationship with you, Lord and the atmosphere created and produced. Lord, may my walk and conversation produce in me the character of Jesus and may they form on the line of the precepts of Jesus Christ as the Holy Spirit applies them to my circumstances. Oh prove thy consciousness in me oh Lord. Lord, I buried my 'stick' so weak or strong I am going to do your will and doubt itself. The devil does not have a grip on my personality. I am indeed free of individuality and emancipated out into personality. I live consecrated energy and sanctified. My arrows of victory have fallen straight in the desert. I do not need to live a patched-up personality any more. Thank-you God for the supernatural equipment that enables me today. Help me today to be a slave of righteousness for holy purposes. Help me bear fruit that endures to be fruitful but also fruitful in Christ – like character. Oh Lord, take my might have-been and build me a future. Please rearrange my mental furniture around you Lord. May I use even my one talent? Oh Lord, I let go of the resulting clutter of stress in my mind. I now do less well – I stop and recharge. I enjoy what I have already accomplished and I don't owe anyone. Lord, may I not let worldly values infect my godly values. Correct me so my outlook is godly. I fall on my knees in repentance. I walk on in your love. May I enthrone you in my life, King Jesus? May I discern wrong spirits and test them. Lord, I turn to you and know you will never let me go. I can rest my weary soul in you and give you back the life I owe. You love me now your love is ever steadfast. You create and you do sort my whole life out. Like in Joshua I speak to you and 'the sun stopped stock still.' It's incredible. You create and give me back the years and turn it

around into good. You alone are my source of living hope. Amen.

(A prayer that you can clean the darkest sins and wash me white as snow)

26. Oh Lord, I draw a line now as I am finally home! A clear path on which I lay the right tracks as I lay them, your immense power comes on which I can run on to glorify your name. If we lay our tracks the same power that raised Jesus from the dead can and does push us forward. Now is the beginning of everything. Oh Lord, this is it – and what I bind on Earth can be loosened in heaven to bless me. I'm so grateful (Amos 3 v3) those that walk with me agree to walk through these times together. Oh Lord, I have slain and now drag it into the light, like Abraham who finally believed (Genesis 20 v17) and trusted you. Thank you, you are a God of the suddenly God. You pass by with a miracle and I am out of the tree of my deepest sins: Realising at the end of self is the beginning of everything. All that lurking fear is now dragged into the light, the stuff that sniffs in cold corners that comes out in at midnight, at 3.0am. I don't need to fight against the goads. I live in your chosen work for me, surrender my desires the difference now being that my will is broken, which means my soul can be coloured and released. You Lord, stayed up all night and drove back my Red Sea and bought me out of my night. I bind my sin on the altar, Lord, and I live in quiet dignity at the beginning of everything. Oh Lord, I bind it all to the horns of the altar. I am gripped by God's love alone. He indeed fills up my horizon. The old man is in the desert, the skin is shed. What God has not started, yes all attachments are indeed burnt up. Amen.

(A prayer that you enlarge me in distress)

27. Lord, may I indeed practice the presence of God that I need to keep my roots so deep, so grounded. Oh Lord, when you shine through me so that lives are drawn to you. May I stay rooted to you deeper than myself in habit, silent, secret

conversation of my soul with you God? May my interaction with you Lord make others want to know you? Lord, you never let me settle but ever test me – you enlarge me when I was in distress (Psalm 4 v1). I learn so much about the person you want me to be when I go through these awful trials. Lord, may I be accountable for behaviour that I do need to change that I will move on when I am meant to. Lord, you take me from distress, lack of purpose and loss of identity, through the pressure of this supreme climb. From the distress into liberation and onto abundance. Yes Lord, it is indeed a Damascus road experience. I am so, so wanted by God. Lord, may I indeed line up the abundance of life in you. I do indeed leave the old man in the desert but I know that only by my being in this desert can I see the vision as the horizon, only that expanse of horizon, to reveal the vision is found in the desert. Amen.

(A prayer of thanks)

28. Oh Lord, thank you that you have given me time to repent and you will, in no wise, fail me. That your banner over me is love. I am indeed out of the furnace and like liquid gold, you met me, restored me, and you build me up into who I truly am. I am not a 'coin' like the parable but like the shekel I am found. Yes you found me. I am your daughter and oh Lord, may I not be disobedient to the heavenly vision. Oh Lord, the shutters are now open and I have been bought into the light. May I marry my gifts with God's in which I was made to live? May I find my stride? I walk away from my past and I am indeed willing to walk away from things that don't belong in my life. Oh Lord, I am at the end of myself and am at last rooted in reality and am secure in God. Oh use my hands and my feet, May I lay 'it' down. May my conduct and character, behaviour and conversation be the Lord's alone? Lord, like Isaiah 11 v2, I am anointed, all that the devil set up is realigned to heal the broken hearted. I am in joy and beauty and allowed the Holy Spirit, his glory rests on me. Oh may my disposition live out the laws of Christ, the hooks are gone, and the natural man is indeed left in the desert. Amen.

(A prayer lest I forget what you have done)

29. Lord, may I not forget the marvellous miracle of what you have done for me. May I run disciplined and experience life in your fullness of real joy. May I let go of self-rejection and to know how valuable I am to you. I do not run in confusion, the shadows have gone and I now know who I am. I don't need to be addicted to fear. I can live on my level and don't need to fight a war in my mind and not sleep when it is time for harvest. I do have everything to live for in you. Like a bridge I am totally fixed. You called me by name Lord and I do come out my tree like Zacharias. I am obedient and changed. I do not need to climb the ladder that does not go anywhere, and I know lord that you tip me over for a reason. You organise a series of events to cause my life to find you. Thank you are my comforter you promise and I can trust you in your strength. I can encourage as you lift my attitude and give me hope. I do not need to live in anxious behaviour. I walk down the corridor of my life yesterday and see pictures of my past. I now do not need to give my power away and I never need to stop hoping. I am not a slave to my thoughts.

(A prayer I walk in the inspiration of my vision)

30. Thank you so much for my vision and that I can walk in the inspiration of my vision until it accomplishes itself. May I not get too practical so I forget the vision? Jesus you want me to be someone I never thought I could be, and live a life so much greater than I could think of. Oh your Gethsemane grief took all the old rags of death cloths and gave life a reason. May I have the courage to truly live so now I know the truth that has set me free? Lord I do not need to give away my powers but dwell on whatsoever things are lovely. May I never again live in false security? Oh lord the passion of knowing you compels me as you feed me and addictions are destroyed. May I reach the place where you can reveal things to me where I have gained enough insight and I can see you shout to me 'It is finished'. This shout has crashed

through all the years to me even in the now. Thank you lord I can crash on your heartbeat. Amen.

(A prayer that I stay in balance)

31. Oh lord, your way is not always popular – it may be against the current but things in my life are either wings or weights. Oh let not sin beset me, the peace you give is truly not found in this world, most people have to wait for a holiday to feel any feeling of peace but Lord, you give us that sun and beach feeling all the time. If we gave you a chance, we can be at peace at all times. May I have the rainbow within an ever-sure light and promise? I sing in gratitude Lord, like Isaiah 54 v1-4. Let me am able to praise you into all areas of my life for in you alone I have hope. Lord, I don't need to give the devil a grip on my personality. My body need not rule me. I can use my gifts to enjoy them. May I stay in your truth, not the feelings? I release the patterns of your love, courage and patterns of your learnt behaviour. Life is not all a rush with crazy coincidences, rather there is a perfect pattern and rhythm with you. Lord, there is definitely a way to go. Lord, may I take what I have learned in life and bring it all to you in your experience. Can I find what good judgment is? You care so much for me. Lord I am made in your image. I am grateful in these moments of revelation. That in you, in the middle of my 'now' that you define me and at the end is a full stop of truth that I don't need to create fears in my imagination, that the truth is in your words. That I can use the same power that raised Jesus from the dead. Amen.

(A prayer that I overcome)

32. I say no to false securities. Oh Lord, sheep are lead, never driven. I am engraved on the palm of God's hand. I am ever before Him. I can stay delivered. I just need to get up and walk! Lord, I am home healed, just one touch and you take all my diseases, all my aching, loneliness. Lord, inverted pride is fear. May I live a life of worship? May I just laugh out loud at the devil's attacks? No more inner perplexity as I live in the

enjoyment of God's friendship. May I see any perplexities in the light of the certainty? May I live in what I do know which is indeed truth. May I keep my hands on the plough? Get up and go from places and thoughts where there is just no safety there anymore. Faith pleases you God. Hope pleases my soul and love sets others free! Oh may I resist and come into an overcomer. Indeed I am truly healed and live such a sane living of life. Amen.

(A prayer I will not be led away)

33. God, you do speak in words and they are life. May I not throw away my confidence? May I not shrink back and shake in the corner all my days. May I never again compromise you? May I try, ever so much harder, to make God's call of me a permanent experience like an athlete to be in strict discipline. Lord, I know that I am tempted in the areas of my strengths where I am indeed strongest. There will be the 'test.' Lord, may I know the joy of accomplishment (Prov 15 v12). You have delivered me and lanced me. I am clutter free. Please God, help the prosperity of my soul, my inner soul be strengthened. Guide my going out and coming in, Lord, you alone have set me free from cycles and patterns of fears and all traits, all worthless traits and manners of my ancestors so I can truly be me. Any of these storms, you alone pull me out of. Lord, like Joseph did with his brothers if I feel you are not there, it is only that you turn your face away so I don't see the tears you're shedding. Oh may I realise just how much you care. May I have the right mindset so like I can see what to avoid and step over! Amen.

(A prayer that I see the way clearly)

34. Thank you God that my life now is upside down and I realise that in the right humbleness, it is the right way up. You have forgiven me and it is over. It need not be brought up again. Lord, I do let go, I disown the sin. I don't justify it. I don't need to think like that. May I gird up my mind? I choose in a deliberate act to go forward on God's word. It is in these

moments of life using my whole will that I live and all the rest is existence. Like invisible gas, I just don't let negative thoughts in. Despite the shocks and challenges, it is staying realigned to God's will. Only then am I in truth. The world and the devil are paralysed when I go God's way and act on his word. I thank you Holy Spirit, that you are in charge of my past and you use me unconsciously. So I have the courage to live this risen life, may I use the conscious part of my body that I am responsible for in a way that glorifies your name. May my conscious life not live in grey areas anymore? The giants are way too big to miss! I can nail my past self to the door. I never need to be deceived by the subtlety of the devil. My Christian faith is a permanent experience. Oh Lord, the beyond has come within me and risen to the above. All I have to do is believe. Amen.

(A prayer that I walk with you)

35. Lord, I am not 'home' yet! May I sow in the spirit and indeed reap the harvest and not lose heart. Oh Holy Spirit, you interpret in my subjectivity what Jesus did objectively, that the freedom is the authority. Oh I never want to go back to my Egypt. I am now under the yoke of Jesus and don't wistfully return to bondage and don't make my own golden calf! Like a vomit, may I do it quickly and get out all the bad in me. May I realise just what God actually does when I choose to believe Him. He moves all my mountains to be there for me. Look at His mighty works! I present my case to the Lord in His court. I can renounce the deceitful things, all hidden things, and all small and great things that are not of you. I can now stand up inside and start my road home, out of the desert to meet you on your holy hill. I am stamped with God's identity. I do now know my destination. You are my only habit, now Lord. I consecrate all to you. May I live consecrated energy and sanctified. Oh Lord, like a candle trim my wick in all little ways. It has cost you everything for you to go and make a home for me. May I not compromise or line up a cheap half-life when you have given me a full life. I shed the old garments. I stretch out my hand and get up and go. Amen.

(A prayer for a healed mind from deep anxieties)

36. Lord, lift me high on your shoulders. I want to see more. Let me not live in my current or a limited perspective anymore, for you have intentions for me. Let me not overlook what you intend for me, that you do lean down and enter my life to make it more meaningful, not harder. Let me always be in awe of you. Lift me up and show me, Lord, the move I was made for. Lord, I know you have a picture of my future and I know that you bless me indeed. Lord, you lift me out of the ordinary and you do grant my requests. As I look through the scriptures, I do see that specific verses pinpoint a need in my life at that moment. Lord, I am in the midst of things yet you do give me the supernatural equipment to deal with it all. Lord, despite my hesitations do remove the borders, remove the limits, enlarge my place in the world so I can be of significance and be purposeful. Lord, may I recognise your call, if you are asking me to step up, to actually 'buy the field', to just go with the amazing encounters and acknowledge it is your agenda, not mine. Lord I bring only what I have. Give me wisdom. I cry out for your hand to guide me, for your hand to be on me in that intimate loving touch. To know that you are indeed there in my moment of need. Lord, may I not ignore you but let you be active in my everyday life. May I walk in the spirit and be led by the spirit and be filled with the spirit. Pray I have boldness as I know your hand on my life is just so powerful. Thank you for being that near. May I know that breakthrough into dependence and that you Lord, are not limited by my weaknesses but because of my weaknesses, you get liberated in my life. You get to reveal your amazing power. I believe and trust you to do what is humanly impossible as I am who I am (Ex 3 v14, John 8v58). Yes Lord, you are: God, you are the "I am". Oh like Esther, may I know that I am here for such a time as this. I rely on God to come through for me. Lord, I am now safe to succeed as you keep me from evil. Lord, may I play my part and 'keep away', not to 'go there' Lord, Satan will tempt me where I am not on guard. May I acknowledge the areas that are vulnerable and

take proactive, preventative measures to avoid being tempted? Protect my attitude, my thought life and my responses to others. May I walk away from temptations I face that you, Lord, will make a way of escape? May I believe the truth, not a lie? Let scripture restore God's truth to my mind. May I state out loud what is true? So that Satan cannot argue. I do not have a spirit of fear. I attack the lie by stating the truth. May I take my thoughts captive, humble myself and renew my mind. Lord, you sometimes halt and I can get my priorities straight and my life in balance. May my walk with you be what it was meant to be, the most exciting experience of my life and how you turn what was meant to be, into what is. May I enjoy the parade now I'm out of the pigsty and back home? Amen.

(A prayer that I run into my future)

37. Lord, cover my life with your fingerprints. Your divine hand has touched my life. Lord, my lifelong habit is beginning each day with the expectations of seeing the supernatural. I come with desperation and I trust that the course of my life will shift! I do not need to live needlessly with cancelled sins, like expired food. It isn't life in you. I am here all along, your blessings are already waiting for me. This golden thread runs right through scripture and my backbone. Lord, life in you is a lifestyle of miracles. May I be a holy asker? Lord, you care not where I started from but where I ended up. With your favour, I reach for another kind of life with a new name as I am called by you. May today, I cast away all the doubts that limit your goodness. May I be on fire with holy ambition? Lord, I see the horizon you have given me, we all die under the same sky and I see the expanse. May I run and run into the vision and as I run out of my first wind, realise I actually have a second. The energy that is lined to the dreams in me, amazes me. Lord, you have prepared my life in advance. May I not cower in fears that hinder me but are based on an untruth that fear doesn't have that much power over me anymore. The truth is what matters. Give me that mountain. Oh Lord, may I pray God-sized prayers. May I walk and meet

the miracle with my name on it. May I put truth to work in my life? May the truth change the way I act and think. Oh Lord, may I move into my huge new life. May the size of my faith match the size of your destiny for me? May I never put you in a box? May I consciously commit my work to your glory? May I improvise on your clear instructions? Lord, may I trust you enough to know any sin cannot fully overpower me as you always give me a way out and bring sin into the full glare of truth. May I not look for the right things in the wrong places? Lord, the temptation recedes into the darkness, far from my senses and the pull of sin fades as you, and you alone, meet my deepest needs. May I be on my guard from the roar surprise of the lion's breath and that one unprepared, quick jab that could cause me to sin? May I actively pursue your favour today with watchfulness, humility, faithfulness, a clear conscience and a great hope? May I be a vessel for honour, sanctified and useful? I do not need to be burdened by injuries of the past or old accusations. Lord, may I not have recurring sin but live in God-honouring ways. This is the beginning of my new identity accomplished and ready. May I never look back but go anywhere as long as it is forward! Amen.

(A prayer that I am free from lusts of the flesh)

38. Lord, you have taken care of the vertical changes with my identity and destiny but may I be more responsible to obey you in the horizontal sphere of my life. Lord, slavery to sin results in a death like existence. Lord, sin only can strangle hold me in this temporal condition, not change my position in Christ and my eternal destiny and identity. May I not be like Ananias and keep things from you and be like Hannah, pray despite the impossible? May I not keep riches that belong to you for I give you my all and you return some things on the water? I live the non-negotiable today. Lord, I am my own person at last, stronger on my knees. You have stood me up. Like Nebuchadnezzar, I fell down and ate grass like cattle and in the middle of anything on any day, the peace does reign.

The peace can stay in the middle of everything in my day. No more chaos. No more extremes in reactions, emotions, words. Lord, you have indeed planted a hedge around me. Lord, may I go the narrow way, put a hedge around my morality, help me to be open, creative and delight in you. Lord and who I really am alone. Don't let lust grab hold of my mind again. Please help me stay sanctified, as the 'jigsaw is fixed.' Help my impact with the world, not come from chaos but calm, order, sanity. Like Joseph, help me to count the cost of my actions and realise the consequences. I live my heavenly birthright, my soul is safe, my will, mind and emotion return to their blueprint. I put on the breaks of old habits. I am a new creation. Help me this year to have good friends I am accountable to. Help my insides to be so in tune I can discern wrong notes. Help me not to be divided against myself in areas of my life, like money and friends. I choose to change my mind. I am in the palace and the parade. I am out the pigsty of abuse. Amen.

(A prayer that I stay true to who I am)

39. The realest me Lord, is attached to the vine and I do not need to give my branches away. Lord, I just give away the fruit. I live an uncompromising, committed to holiness. Lord, I strive to be holy. Help me to sense the sin and fear and recognise it is dark, dangerous and damnable! May I get my life clean and keep it clean and to know when to do a complete inner cleansing periodically of thoughts, habits, motives. May I throw out any 'leaven' that clutters up or puts blockages up in my life? Sensitise me to hidden sins. May I recognise doubt causes me to sin and deception causes me to be disobedient and that causes spiritual death? Lord, only in recognition of your sovereignty and in the reality of personal responsibility that to obey your commands and your principles, May I conduct myself and construct my life as I am an active participant in the building of God's kingdom. May I recognise, not just observe, and accept and embrace, guide not guess, fulfil rather than dream, perfectly conclude rather than live, in blind hope. May I get up and go where there is no

safety anymore. Now I am sane, may I think sanely? Lord, help my reason to have returned now you are my sovereignty. Lord, I embrace your right of control and help me to reason theologically. May I be on my guard so I am not carried away by the errors of unprincipled men? I draw near with confidence to the throne of grace. Amen.

(A prayer to face my giants)

40. Lord, as my giants move close to attack, may I run quickly to meet them! I run at my giant today for he is not all I see. I discuss it only with you, Lord, as I see the more of you. Lord, I seize the moment and defeat that giant. I load my sling and swing at it, my heart might but patchy. Lord, but you see the realest me. The battle is the Lord's and you will give it into my hands. Thank you even if I run from you, in the past you still have my place reserved only for me and once I accept the call, I am indeed home. I don't need to be stalked anymore by the devil. Lord, no one to abuse, seduce, belittle me. I am in your friendship circle. You, my soul mate, protect me, you seek nothing but my interests, and you seek nothing but my happiness. Thank you lord you search the world for me. You will sift the chaff and keep the grain. I have a covenant with you. I wonder freely now in your goodness, memories may press on my mind but they don't control me anymore. I am not alone with them anymore. I look at what I have in you. Despite the noises or people around here in the middle of friendship, with you my heart is in tune. Amen.

(A prayer against loneliness even with other Christians)

41. Lord, is it so easy to feel condemned, to sit in the pews at church and feel just so isolated and awkward. May I know your grace moves my mental furniture around and back into place? May I trust in your truth and not consider or snatch at a mistruth, to hang on to a lie, just to gain some assurance that has no solid foundation to it all. Lord, in this day and age it is so often that the gospel is watered down, that as Christians we

live in the grey area. May we re-find and refine our holy living. To know that any spot or stain can defile the whole batch. May I never lose my God focus? May I know that you are my more than enough? Lord, may I not take that path again of a truth-shading desperation. I want to hold up the truth that is my only weapon against a sarcastic, inconsistent world. Lord, I rest in your compassion that Lord, the love of Jesus can be shown by those in the church who understand grace and know the truth of the word of God in all its black and white. I pray they will see the shades of grey of a foolish Christian who has sinned and help sort the right and wrong. I pray for Christians who live by your wisdom that they can guide those who feel alone back into beautiful fellowship. Lord, you do give me bread of life and you take away my desperation. Amen.

(A prayer to come out the cave of shame)

42. Lord, the land is so barren, everything I've tried to plant has died or dried up. It is a 'given up' plot, a barren soul Lord stripped! Lord, I know when I'm in that place as I can't see you despite there being absolutely nothing to block my vision. I can't see you, Lord! All I see is the trouble and I'm in danger of trying to sort it out completely on my own. Is it in those times of isolation that I scurry into a place that seems safe, silent and shady? Lord, I have willingly found my own caves and lain down exhausted in the dirt and closed my eyes for a decade! Lord, I've put on so many acts, played so many roles, and gone a little crazy for the shows of being accepted by the crowd. Lord, how many of us stand at the entrance to the cave and think, as we look out on a horizon limited by the arch above us of the cave opening, just what will we do now. Lord, give me the courage to leave this cave of all my habits and refocus on you, my refuge and strength. May I come out of the cave and see the expanse of the horizon and how you, indeed, enlarge me when I am in distress. You are all I need. I realise this when I find out you are all I have. Oh Lord, I go from folly such foolishness, to such loneliness and only then do I re-find you, you are my only restoration. I have been in

the desert cave for way too long. Lord, I have squeezed out droplets of acid pain, fermented over years. Now I am restored and the words blossom so sweetly, there is a landscape again. Amen.

(A prayer to put on God Glasses)

43. Lord, may I have a God dominated mind. Lord, I know the roots of the truth of my salvation are deeper than any thoughts or negative thoughts or actions. These roots have endured and they go deeper, that being vindicated or being proved right. Lord, I don't need to feed the savage thoughts and fertilise the rampaging insecurities. Oh may you dominate over and above the emotions of offense and fear as I go that much deeper to the source. Lord, I can view all things on the surface through the lens, the frame of heavens, Lord, and it doesn't need to be about me at all. I belong to you and that is my hope. All my enemies are your projects. Lord, I hand them over and it or they doesn't need to consume me at all. I forgive and don't translate forgiving as excusing or pretending. May I not gloss over or side step another's sin but face it, yet also keep my distance. I don't need to live in the same space. I do not forgive in foolishness. I forgive as then I move on and I can't think about it anymore. I don't excuse or endorse or embrace those who hurt me. I just reroute my journey here on this Earth through heaven. My enemies are God's child and I accept grace in my life so I also share it. I feel so free now I have forgiven. I have met my source. My roots go much deeper than any bomb site. Amen.

(A prayer to be beautiful)

44. Lord, thank you. Your tone is the tune of my day. I am in your beauty, even amongst the 'beasts' of my day. I am free from their destructive grip, all of selfishness, hatred and pride. They no longer have the last word. Lord, hope still stirs in me. I live by a higher code despite the barbaric behaviour around me. I offer the right words to diffuse, not ignite. I bring beauty where it is unexpected. Lord, may my gentleness reverse

torrents of anger and aggression. May my soft words be weight enough to crush all opposition? Lord, whoever I have in my life who is hard to stomach, I stop staring at them. I shift my gaze to Jesus. I look at my mediator, not the troublemakers. May I get the best of evil by doing good. May I be the beauty in the middle of the beasts and see what happens. Amen.

(A prayer to have God on speed dial)

45. Lord, I keep your number on speed dial. I won't immerse myself in this fear and let it take over. Lord, you have anointed me. You have given me a promise, an assurance and you assure my safety through this time. May I not just lie in the pastures and backyard of the devil 'compromising' and limiting all that I am. Lord, in this 'going through' time, I want to handle it correctly. Lord, when hope takes the last train and joy is the name of a girl and when I'm so tired of trying and forgiving and of hard work and of Lord-headed people, Lord, may I not look in the cul-de-sacs to try re-energise my life. Lord, all that does is numb the pain, not remove it. May I not jump blindly off the cliff or crash into a place with again, no solutions! Oh may I never forget to pray. May I seek healthy counsel? May I go through it knowing despite the fog there is a shoreline waiting just for me? May I take one more step to do it one more time, encourage one more soul? I will find strength in the Lord, my God. It is so good to be back! Amen.

(A prayer for rest)

46. Oh Lord, you give me such blessed rest. Oh, I have been burnt so much by the roaring lion's breath of surprise! By the demands that are too constant. Lord, you enable me a place of rest for my worn-out self. Lord, I can just sit and rest. It is at the Brook Besor I can stay. It is a place of rest you give to me. Help me see where it is and to allow myself such rest. Thank you that you dignify my decision to stop and rest when others go on and do mighty deeds. Lord, you fight when I

can't and the battle is indeed the Lord's. May I know your rest when I'm just too tired to fight and too ashamed to complain. Thank you that you bless rest. Amen.

(A prayer of peace in my loss)

47. Thank you, you give us a time to mourn. Lord, it is in this time that I refine, after such depths of grief. I now can give myself time to face it. Lord, I can now face the grief as the grave is not the last word. I haven't just lost at a board game or misplaced my keys. I can't walk away from such grief, it is real. I flush it out – with it comes the enormity of anxiety and of guilt and of wistfulness and of forgetfulness and of suicidal thoughts. Lord, I lament. Yes Lord, even in your word, you say through such sorrow we can be refined. Lord, I weep and I worship you. I allow myself to weep. I face it and give myself a time to mourn. Lord, I know I have hope as you are a God of resurrection. Only in you is there a hope and future despite the finality of sorrow, grieving and death. Lord, I weep as creatively as I worship. Amen.

(A prayer for wisdom)

48. Lord, I want a conscience void of offense, a heart cleansed in the blood of Christ and a spiritual nature filled with the Holy Spirit. Lord, in this world of massive size questions, may I inquire of you Lord. May I get up and know just where to go. May I always run my opinions past you? Lord, like the ephod of the priests, the stones Urim and Thummim, I may not have them but I have a Bible that tells me and I get alone with you Lord, where the lights and shadows of the Earth cannot interfere, where self-will doesn't intrude, where human opinions cannot touch. Lord, you love me too much to have me wander – your Holy Spirit dwells in me and may my 'want to' feelings follow you. Lord, I know when I have no peace over something and I praise you when I know you're in a decision and I feel right about it. May I select the way that is good? May I heed my heart for you Lord? Lord, you speak through my conscience. In your word,

verbs dart back and forth across the page. You reach deep within me with your word. The word of God stirs a sigh from my soul. Amen.

(A prayer to shed my old self)

49. Lord, I turn a deaf ear to the old voices, to the crocodile who lurks in the stagnant water at the bottom of my soul. I press the mute button on all those bullies. Lord, may I listen attentively to your words about me. May I live in the correct fear that praises, loves, worships and adores you? May I draw a line in the sand and kick up my heels. May I dance in the sand as your presence is my arch of the sky, limitless and complete? You are not fitted into any box-like shape. May I have the correct reverence, awe and fear so I do not live in the limits of my own fearful perception of you. Thank you that in revering you, I can find a dance and a song to sing. Lord, you dance with me. Amen.

(A prayer that I come up higher)

50. Lord, you are a complete rainbow promise. I can sit in heavenly places right now! Despite all my broken promises, you keep yours to me always. Lord, your promise is enduring despite circumstances. You will always burst into colour despite any grey days. Your promises are forever, Lord, as you seat me in heavenly places. You promised me eternal life before the word begun. Thank you for keeping the lights on so I can see my way home. May I understand your love? May I know real love and loyalty and act out real love and do what real love does. May I see those that need me and not lose control of my self-control and may I keep my vision nearest. Lord, press me hard; burst the seeds out of my fruit. Let me get up and go from where there is no safety anymore. Lord, in all I do, I can say 'But God' you are the answer at the end of the echo – you are what comes back and can make it all meant for good. You take my plans, you interrupt my life and because of what you do in my life, I can say 'yet God.' Amen.

(A prayer that you paint my canvas)

51. Lord, I ran through the valley soaked in you in my will, mind and emotions. May I look after your reputation as my life is a blank canvas and people will see the painting I paint? However, with your colours, it can be an example of a miracle life. May I face you and with you, face the trials. Lord, you have taken the past I do not remember. All I have is the victory call of you despite the type of life I lived then. Despite the past, the life is won. It is hid with God. The devil can't find it! Thank you. My thought life is fixed indeed, mended and it is tuned in to you. On this white canvas, the outline is drawn in the shadow of your hand I rest. The darkness only defines the shape more. Without that dark past of fears, what outline could I present to the world. Thank-you Lord, you use me as a showcase. God shows his grace, his mercy and he shines. He is the colours of my life. Thank you. Your sacrifice is my dot to dot, my sin may be so dark but you can use that outline and fill it with the tremendous colours that match and make me. My picture makes sense and comes alive in your hands. There are no gaps as you paint me whole. You never miss the mark. You never colour outside the outline you define for me. Because of you, I am framed and in a position of presence and the place meant for me all along. Amen.

(A prayer I obey you fully)

52. Lord, I recognise consequences. There is a moral law within me that holds me up. Who else has that 'coat hanger' on which to hang all their emotions, hopes and fears. To have that shape so perfectly whole, so truly complete is such a feat in an insecure world. I know most of my life Lord, I have broken myself against the laws. Who was I to ever think I could break the laws. Only myself broke and shattered those most precious stones and jewels of my identity. My disposition was dented and scratched in the process of stumbling through the jungle of life, unarmed with logic, self-esteem and wise guidance. It's amazing that I have found myself out of the other end of it all. I have come out from under the laws of this world and found you have put a stamp

on my nature, a texture to my human heart. Your laws are carved into my heart to make me the person I am already meant to be with you! Lord, you have drained my reservoir and cleared out all the debris. For to be in your will is so much better than success. For me to be in God's will is success for it is me, it is you, that is the real excellence of my life. Lord is truly interwoven and can only really result from right living. People yearn for so much they will do anything even 'lick the Earth' as Pascal said, but oh my Lord, I sit at the foot of the cross and let you unfold me inside out. Amen.

(A prayer I come back to my first love)

53. Oh Lord, may I believe in the first love of the soul. May I not ever now put my soul in peril? Lord, place a hedge around me. May I recognise how you lift all that bends and breaks me? You take all the inner compulsions and the pressure of circumstances. Lord, may I know the difference between the urgent and the important. May I live in an awareness of my spiritual life at the atmosphere of my spirit in a holy awe to know I live and breathe at one with God? May my life spread your loveliness like a flower gently opening and releasing all its perfume? Thank you that I can hear my heart's song inside. I can feel the light and life fully flowing, fully glittering that I am so healthy in my inner life as you have furnished, redecorated, renovated it to perfection! Lord, you do such a good job on me. You, in love, truly crush all I am. All I did, you just take it down and what you build in its place is so magnificent. Look what you have done for me. Jesus did this change in me. Lord, may I sit consistent, no more spasms and jerks to every seduction that comes my way. Lord, may I look to you so whatever ingratitude faces me, nothing devastates my soul as I am set on God's ride through the dark, damp underbelly of the world. Amen.

(A prayer to praise you in the mornings)

54. Each day I wake, Lord. I count as many blessings as I can. I quietly wake in that thought. I draw near to the good

things, whatsoever is lovely, so I am in health in my mind and heart. I consciously recognise, despite any business of my day, your intervening hand in my life. I have a deep, settled peace in my soul despite. Thank you for all those in my life that have shown me mercy. I am so grateful that I now do not take anything for granted. I now trawl through the index of my life and the journals and the diary and highlight all the good things that have happened. My heart is so full to brimming and I am spontaneously kind to God. I put my soul on charge to regenerate it so it is active and on, in all I say and do. My will stirs up my mind. Whatever I feel, Lord, I praise you! I command my mind, despite all, to focus on reasons to praise you. As a writer, Lord, when I stop it is because my pen has run out, not my praise for you. I know that the coincidences in my life are in the light of providence. They are God given moments as you, Lord, are at work in us in ways beyond our understanding. May we recognise the spiritual blessings! I trace every good and perfect gift back to you, Jesus. What you allow, Lord, you can also use. May I ask you each day what will you give me today that I can offer back to you? When I can't work out what has happened to me, thank you God, you can. I can't wait to see how you turn this into good! Amen.

(A prayer that I exercise my faith)

55. Lord, I truly do keep on keeping on, as I never give in except to convictions of honour and good sense. I never have given up Lord and my soul is so fortified for the task I live out permanent perseverance and persistence, as my soul is strong at last. Like a handle, I hold on so tightly, Lord, to the truth. Lord, I'm glad for the discipline of living through this universe to know you have the power to dissolve into nothing all that seems too large for me to cope with. May my doubts not harden me into unbelief and just create more boulders that I will have to clear out of my way, once I come back to the knowledge of the truth. I stand up to Satan, Lord, in the name of Jesus and he has to go! I am strong at the broken places because of you. I do not indulge my doubts, Lord, but

compare their colours against the certainty of God's word. How dull and fake they are compared against such bright flesh colours of truth. May I delight in doing your will, Lord Jesus? So please May I gain a more firm moral resolve. Indeed, I have put my hand to the plough. I am not playing anymore at being a Christian but that I live in a resolute will, recognising strenuous stern discipline. I keep on keeping on, especially praying through loneliness and the anxious hours. Oh Lord, may I never live sloppy any more. May I also not get into a rut? I get up every day Lord and I do not meet reflection but meet with you. I greet this present moment as I am so upheld on the inside. Amen.

(A prayer that I can forgive)

56. Lord, I let go. I forgive. I remember now Lord, to forget memories cannot overwhelm me anymore. You have taken the sharp edge off the bitter memories, the cutting acuteness of those feelings have passed. I get rid of such poison in Jesus' name. I make up my mind today. Lord, I bring my will in line with God's will. I have come out of the cul de sac. Oh Lord, I recognise how much I myself have been forgiven. I let the magnanimity of that act reach my heart. May I not never live the longest journey, the 18 inches from my head and my heart? Oh may I so have the realisation of forgiveness. Oh Holy Spirit, help me comprehend the wonder of the fact my debt is paid in full, and you ever so gently turn my life around. The complete rainbow in the sky is so phenomenal yet Lord, my soul is wrapped in a complete rainbow of all your promises to me. The storm of my life for a season is over and peace is in my heart. Lord, you wash the sands of all the shores each day. You fill our world with provisions, with miracles, that we could never do or create. You have washed the shores and you have washed away all my memories. How wonderful is that fact. I lie on the shore of my life Lord, and let you take all the grit out of me so I can be a vessel of your peace and pour peace into this world. Amen.

(A prayer for strength to live alone)

57. Lord, I am not meant to be alone in this world. I can recall even childhood memories which include the unity of togetherness. Lord, may I learn to serve others not by being manipulated or naïve when situations need to be unplugged but that I might truly flourish in all the personality you have given to me. Lord, relationships are the essence of reality and the reason for our existence. I want to learn the right relationships with you and all who are, by fate and circumstances, active in my life. May I keep my backbone consistent of God, myself and others? To fully love even myself, not a love of self but a self-love, not divorced from the equal love of others and not sought for in its own sake at all. May I not draw away from intimacy with you? Lord, may I not be indifferent to you. May I have willingness, the right desire and attitude to serve better? Lord, I choose to serve. I know true life is found in giving. Help me do the good I ought to do and know I should do. May all I do be a blessing as only you can save us. Lord, I confidently leave all in your hands. May I give myself to others as you met needs and may I live a life so worth doing, fully alive, awake in the light of truth. Amen.

(A prayer to live transformed)

58. Lord, when I turn to you, I am not alone at all. I know you came into my heart and rewire it. You turn it on and I realise my reason for being here. Lord, each day I repent as I continually work through to your best instead of my good. Lord, like a caterpillar forming into a butterfly, it is through the struggles, the metamorphosis of struggle that makes me fly. May my life make me truly fly for you, Lord, my repentance is like an earthquake that is in my soul. I see reality without you Lord, I can see a change in the way I see things as you have entered and changed my soul. I have such a revelation of your love for me Lord. May I have an equal revulsion against the sin in my life? May I experience a sorrow that leads to repentance? Sin looks like a different thing to me now. May I let you grip hold and yank that sin out

of me? Lord, I do not want to deteriorate. May each day I abide in your life. May I stop abiding in something else? It is so easy when our souls are in pain, to collect other lovers for our souls. Yet may I let you knit my life together for you know every hinge, every hair. I do try to work independently of you Lord, yet it in produces splinters in my soul. Only in you am I the fullest me. Lord, I hang out with you. I look to you for life. My Good can never be your best for me. I cannot hold your best in a broken cistern and you offer me whole, filled to overflowing life. I turn to you, my face sharp flint. I change my mind and walk in your steps carved out for me. I change my mind and fly into life. Amen.

(A prayer I will see the river in my desert)

59. Lord, how many of us have lost our souls. We do so often neglect them and fall into addictions and emotional pain. We experience obsessions and loss of meaning and purpose. Lord, my soul is my thoughts, feeling and will. It bears the meaning of my life and my personality. My soul, Lord, is meant to feel, to tell me of my wrong goals and wrong thinking. Lord, it is the core of my inner life and personality. Lord, may I also not misuse it but to let you, alone, fill that hollow deep inside with a sense of homecoming, a reconciliation. Nothing in this world is on our side. All needs to be twisted before it is of any use at all. Oh Lord, what you formed may I not deform. Nature is full of death and natural tendency is to die in this world. What minister's growth and beauty equally turns and causes decay and death. Lord, may I not be pulled down blinding my reason, paralyzing my will. Help me team up with the Almighty. In daily contact with you, oh Lord, my soul is renewed in the solitude. With you, my Lord, my soul can be full grown. Oh Lord, despite the dried-up patches, may I always meet with you devotionally. That I can pray and sing anywhere as I learnt. Lord, to pray somewhere I put on my breathing apparatus and dive into the stifling world's atmosphere. I am, Lord, not too busy to have a quiet time because that would make me busier than you intended. I am healed in the temperament (and temperature)

of my soul. I establish a daily appointment with you. Lord, I recast my priorities. I lean into you Lord and my heart is filled with the vision of your heart and I am strong to turn and meet the day. Oh Lord, may the stronger, quieter life come flowing in. I store precious fragments, not splintered shards, in my memory of your living world. Oh Lord, chisel in my soul such living forms that go so deep oh that I hear you Lord, as I come through this dry desert. Not the murmurs of self-will but a trained ear that hears you. I disentangle your voice from the nets of others of misguided friendships, of rebellious romance. Your voice forms such a gentle impression as you think through me. I come out on to a higher level. Oh Lord, out of the dry desert up bubbles the life and I slide onto a higher level. You alone are my river through my desert. Amen.